'D'

How to be a bad
birdwatcher

How to be a bad
birdwatcher

To the greater glory of life

SIMON BARNES

Illustrations by Alex Fox

✴ SHORT BOOKS

First published in 2004 by

Short Books

15 Highbury Terrace

London N5 1UP

10 9 8 7 6 5

A CIP catalogue record for this book
is available from the British Library.

ISBN 1-904095-95-X

Printed in Germany
by GGP Media, Poessneck

To my father – the first bad birdwatcher
I ever met. He taught me all he knew.

*I am but mad north-north-west; when the wind
is southerly, I know a hawk from a handsaw.*

Hamlet

Contents

Hobby

1. Not just a nice hobby

What makes the marvellous is its peculiar way
of being ordinary; what makes the ordinary is
its peculiar way of being marvellous.

Orhan Pamuk, *The Black Book*

I am a Bad Birdwatcher.

On the other hand, and taking one thing with another, when it comes to enjoying birds I am world class.

Where shall I start? With the carmine bee-eaters of the Luangwa Valley in Zambia? With the rhinoceros hornbill glimpsed through a gap in the canopy in the rainforests of Borneo? Or with the crested oropendola seen from the pressbox at the Queen's Park cricket ground in Trinidad (when I was being paid to watch Ian Botham)?

No. Let's start in Barnet, on the extreme edge of London. I used to live there. I was going into the centre of London to meet someone, perhaps even to do some work. I wasn't looking for birds. I hadn't even got binoculars; you can't use them in a London pub, not without attracting adverse comment, anyway.

I wasn't looking for birds, but I am always looking at them, you see. Not for reasons of science, or in hopes of a fabulous rarity, or to make careful observations of seasonal behaviour. Just because looking at birds is one of life's greatest pleasures. Looking at birds is a key: it opens doors, and if you choose to go through them you find you enjoy life more and understand life better.

It was a nice day of early summer, the kind of day when a chap's eyes keep turning to the girls who have moulted into their skimpy summer plumage and men wear their jackets on their thumbs. And because it was such a nice day, I thought I'd walk past the common to Hadley Wood train station rather than through the High Street to High Barnet tube. It turned out to be one of my better decisions.

I was going through Monken Hadley churchyard to catch a train that would get me to Oxford Circus (change at Highbury & Islington) in 40 minutes. And there were lots (note scientific precision) of house martins whizzing round and round the church tower.

Perhaps you know all about house martins. Or perhaps you think they are swallows. No matter. They are jaunty and swallow-like and, if you are lucky, they nest under the eaves of your house and leave aromatic trails down the wall and bring joy to your heart on the rare day in spring when they return from their travels.

They are dapper little chaps, navy blue with white bums, and they are one of the sights and sounds of the English summer: doing things like whizzing round church steeples and catching flies in their beaks. Later in the season the young ones take up whizzing themselves, trying to get the hang of this flying business. I always imagine the martin mother saying: Well done, little one. You flew three times round the church tower. Now you've got another flight to try. Cape Town.

Where was I? Monken Hadley church, pausing on my journey to Oxford Street to spend a few moments gazing at the whirligig of martins. It was nothing special, nothing exceptional, and it was very good indeed. Note this: one of the great pleasures of birdwatching is the quiet enjoyment of the absolutely ordinary.

And then it happened. Bam!

Gone.

From the tail of my eye, I saw what I took to be a kestrel. I turned my head to watch it as it climbed, and I waited for it to go into its hover, according to time-honoured kestrel custom. But it did nothing of the kind. It turned itself into an anchor, or the Greek letter psi. Or a thunderbolt.

No kestrel this: it crashed into the crowd of martins like the wrath of God, and almost as swiftly vanished. I think it got one, but I can't swear to it, it was all so fast. And there I was down on the pavement with a bag full of books on my back, uttering incredulous obscenities and prayerful blasphemies. What the hell was that?

It was a hobby. Perhaps the most dashing falcon of them all: slim, elegant and deadly fast. Not rare as rare-bird-addicts reckon things: they come to Britain in reasonable numbers every summer to breed. The sight of a hobby makes no headlines in the birdwatching world. It was just a wonderful and wholly unexpected sight of a wonderful and wholly unexpected bird. It was a moment of perfect drama. Note this: one of the great pleasures of bird-watching is the moments of peak experience.

We humans tend to simultaneous and mutually exclusive desires: to be married, to be single; to be social, to be alone; to travel adventurously, to stay at home.

Birdwatching embraces both halves of our natural desire for contradiction. It brings us enhanced enjoyment of the ordinary, the easy and the safe, and it brings us moments of high drama and gratification and dangerous delight.

Rather like life, really. And that is what bad bird-watching is all about. Life, that is to say.

***

Let's go back to that hobby, and those martins. How much skill was required? How much knowledge? How much scientific background? None, none, and none. The martins were just there, being obvious and making their merry farting calls to each other: one of the great ambient birds of the English summer. Everyone has seen martins, and is aware of them at some level, even if he can't put a name to them and is unaware of the diagnostic white bums.

And the hobby was unmissable, unmistakable: a great black (I saw him only in silhouette) force. It wasn't necessary to identify the bird, to know it by name; it was enough to witness a fierce and terrible drama. Any bad birdwatcher would know it was a bird of prey, and any human being would have known it was something dreadful. Knowing its name was a luxury. It wasn't exciting because it was rare and because I could call it *Falco subbuteo* and because I could tick it and boast about it. It was exciting because it was a thrilling bird in a thrilling moment.

Now, I am lying here just a bit. Knowing that the bird was a hobby was a formal completion of the business. It was an explanation, a key to the drama. That is what hobbies do, you see: they turn into anchors or psis and make sudden lacerating dives into flocks of circling martins. It was gratifying to have the explanation: the understanding.

But before the understanding comes the wonder. Comes the delight. And that is the first aim of being a bad bird-watcher: the calm delight of the utterly normal, and the rare and sudden delight of the utterly unexpected.

The only real skill involved in this perfect birdwatching moment was the willingness to look. It was not skill that gave me the sight; it was habit. I have developed the habit of looking: when I see a bird I always look, wherever I am. It is no longer a conscious decision. I might be in the middle of a conversation of amazing importance about the Direction Of Our Marriage, but my eye will flick out of the window at a hint of movement, caught in the tail of my eye, and I will register: bloody hell, sparrowhawk. I might say it aloud, too – not necessarily a wise decision.

I once found a questionnaire in a birdwatching magazine. It asked: "How often do you go birdwatching?" I reject the question out of hand. I don't go birdwatching. I am birdwatching. Birdwatching is a state of being, not an activity. It doesn't depend on place, on equipment, on specific purpose, like, say, fishing. It is not a matter of organic train-spotting; it is about life and it is about living.

It is matter of keeping the eyes and ears and mind open. It is not a matter of obsession, not at all. It is just quiet enjoyment. A happy married man will still glance at pretty girls and appreciate their loveliness without the need to do anything about it. It is just a habit of heterosexual males to look, and it is one that adds to the gaiety of life.

A car nut will make a quiet, unthinking appraisal of every vehicle he sees; it is part of the way his mind works. He will hardly be aware that he is doing it, unless his glance is caught by something exceptional. The habit is not something to do with what he does; it is something to do with what he is.

And that is what being a bad birdwatcher is all about. It is just the habit of looking. Born-againers talk about Bringing Jesus Into Your Life; this book is an invitation to bring birds into your life. To the greater glory of life.

Woodlark

2. Hamlet was a bad birdwatcher

And all around not to be found...
Gerard Manley Hopkins, *The Woodlark*

Perhaps you know nothing at all about birds. Perhaps you even say it: well, me, I know nothing at all about birds. If so, you are lying through your teeth. It is impossible to know nothing at all about birds. Trust me: you can identify several different kinds of birds. Let's compile a list of birds that you can already recognise – even if you call yourself the most ignorant birdwatcher in the land:

robin

swan

duck

blackbird

swallow

crow

sparrow

blue tit

heron

pigeon

That's ten for a start. Now we'll throw in cuckoo, because that is the one bird that every one can recognise on call. And you might as well add a few more:

thrush

seagull

goose (perhaps even Canada goose)

kestrel

owl

pheasant

eagle

kingfisher

magpie

You can recognise a woodpecker by ear, when you hear

it bashing the hell out of a branch. And of course there are plenty of birds that you can recognise from pictures, without ever being in much danger of seeing: snowy owl (from Harry Potter films), puffin (from the spines of paperback books) and of course, a Famous Grouse. And you could throw in a few exotics, too: parrot, peacock, toucan, flamingo, pelican, ostrich. True, not all the birds in those two lists are proper species. For example, there are three species of swan that you can see in Britain. And please don't be put off when I tell you that there are 74 different species of cuckoo in the world. But we'll bother with species later. Let us keep things simple and talk about different kinds of birds. A swan is a different kind of bird from a robin: and, if you can tell the difference between one kind of bird and another, you have already established your birdwatching credentials. This is something we can all do, as surely as we can tell a car from a lorry.

So there is an awful lot of latent knowledge of birds that most people in this country possess. Birds are part of our common culture. You can concrete over the land, but you can't concrete over our minds. We have our roots in rural soil, even the most urban of us. Birds are part of our lives and our thought processes, whether we acknowledge the fact or not. We are all bad birdwatchers; it is an inescapable part of our lives.

A liking for birds is quite different to a liking for stamps or matchbox labels. I find it hard to believe that people like these things for themselves; they are just a medium for collection mania. True, for some people there are lashings of collection mania involved in birdwatching – it takes the form of making lists rather than actually collecting dead birds – but it is not necessary to be a maniacal collector in order to be a bad birdwatcher, or, for that matter, a good one.

I shall go on to the maniac business in due course. Let us just point out for now that the collection maniacs are not the mainstream. They are not the orthodoxy. They are not even the elite. They are just people who love birds and birdwatching, and are equally ravished by an arcane competitiveness. Some are good birdwatchers, some (but don't ever tell them) are bad birdwatchers. But they are all, to a man (and they are mostly men), great competitors.

Good luck to them. But they are not what all bird-watchers want to be in their heart of hearts. Perish the bloody thought. Perhaps you own a car. There is a kind of car-owner who goes in for mania. He will have a collector's car, a buff's car: say an MGA. And he will love it and make love to it with interminable tinkerings and polishings, and he will drive it (lovingly) to rallies, and he will meet fellow-maniacs, and they will talk about technicalities and parts, and they will talk shop and they will bitch about the people who aren't there. And generally have a lovely time. Ordinary motorists are as much like classic car buffs as ordinary (good and bad) birdwatchers are to the species of birdwatching maniacs known as twitchers.

Mad collectors are all very well. As Miss Jean Brodie said, for those who like that sort of thing, that is the sort of thing they like. So let us leave the collectors on one side for the moment. The point of birdwatching is not bird-watchers but birds.

Birds have always been part of English or British life; not just as things to eat, but as part of the way we see and understand the world. Birds were even used to tell fortunes. Prediction by means of birds is called ornithomancy: the flight of a hawk, the passing of a vee-shaped straggle of ducks might be an evil sign, or it might be the most auspicious omen. In fact, the very word "auspicious" comes from the Latin for birdwatching.

English literature echoes with the sound of birds. In the Anglo-Saxon poem, *The Seafarer*, we hear of the plaintive loneliness of the bad birdwatcher:

Sometimes I made the song of the wild swan
My pleasure, or the gannet's call, the cries
Of curlews for the missing mirth of men...

Probably a whooper swan, I'd reckon. But really, the poor seafarer must have been in a dreadfully low state to imagine the mournful, far-carrying bubbling call of the curlew as an echo of human laughter. If you know the curlew's call, your heart has to bleed for the poor man who heard it and heard the uproar of conviviality.

Hamlet said that he was mad north-north-west: when the wind was southerly, he could tell a hawk from a handsaw. This line has baffled not a few in its time, but handsaw (or hansaw) is a contraction of heronshaw, which means a young heron. Hamlet was clearly a bad birdwatcher himself, though he probably carried a falcon rather than a pair of binoculars when he went a-birding. When the wind was southerly, he could tell the slow rhythmic wing-beat of a young heron from the flap-flap-glide of a hawk. No great trick to that: even a bad birdwatcher like the moody prince was up to it.

Poets have always celebrated birds. William Blake said that robin redbreast in a cage put all heaven in a rage; Gerard Manley Hopkins not only rejoiced in a kestrel in *The Windhover*, the most thrilling nature poem ever written – my God, what would have written had he seen my hobby? – but he also wrote the definitive poem about being a bad birdwatcher, and his problem in telling one lark from another:

Teevo cheevo cheevio chee:
O where, what can that be?

It's a woodlark, Father Hopkins. Lovely song, too. The bird can even sing its own Latin name, or the first part of it: Lullula arborea. The French call it *l'alouette loulou.*

I touch on literature here not for the sake of the poets but for the sake of the birds and the bad birdwatchers. Birds are in our past, they are in our blood and in our bones. In short, when you make the decision to become a bad birdwatcher, you do not start from scratch. You are already a bad birdwatcher. The baddest birdwatcher on the planet starts off with a huge bank of information, tradition and culture. After that, it is just a matter of getting the habit. The habit of looking. And listening, like Father Hopkins, but we will come to that later.

So let us make a start on the looking side of things right now.

Look out of the window.
See a bird.
Enjoy it.
Congratulations. You are a bad birdwatcher.

Barn Owl

3. Birds are only human

'Tis not through envy of thy happy lot,
But being too happy in thine happiness, –
　　　　　Keats, *Ode to a Nightingale*

Why birds? Why not mammals? After all, we are mammals ourselves; it makes more sense to watch our own kind. Or why not reptiles, since reptiles are wonderfully *unlike* our own kind? Or insects, because there are so many more of them to see? Or plants, because they at least have the decency to keep still?

Birds are the most studied organisms on the planet. They are the best observed, the most fanatically recorded, the most lovingly written about. Birds have more good observers than any other kind of animal, and untold millions more bad ones. Why?

The answer is obvious. Because they're obvious. Birds, I mean. At the end of the last chapter, when you looked out of the window, you will have seen a bird all right, unless you were dead unlucky and in absolutely the wrong place and didn't want to look for more than a few seconds, or it was dark and there were no owls passing by.

But how many mammals did you see? I mean, wild mammals? Thought not. It is a rare and generally exciting thing to see a wild mammal.

Squirrels, yes, grey squirrels in the park. Bunnies are easy enough to see, too. But that's it. It's a real thrill to see any wild mammal. Or at least unexpected – not everyone is overjoyed at the sight of a house mouse or *Rattus norvegicus*.

When did you last see a living hedgehog? And hedge-hogs, as we know from their sad, flat corpses, are pretty common. That's because hedgehogs, like most mammals, are creatures of the night. They have their being at times when we light-loving humans are just not around. Or even if we are, it's too dark to see the bloody things.

And how often have you seen a weasel or a stoat? I live in the country these days and spend a lot of time outside.

I saw a deer 300 yards off the other night, because I was carrying an extra powerful torch; and I got a glimpse of a stoat last week. A few nights ago, a hare crossed the road in front of me and performed a spectacular can't-catch-me leap: gorgeous animals. That's three decent mammal sightings in a little more than a week. A pretty satisfying week for casual observation, I reckon.

And birds? Hundreds of sightings and hearings. Birds are always around for bad birdwatchers to be aware of. Wild mammals are exceptional; wild birds are part of daily life.

Then there is the question of the number of species, of different kinds. There are maybe 20 different kinds of mammals you could hope to see on land in this country; as for birds, there are a couple of hundred easily available. The top twitchers have scores beyond 500.

So birds are available to be seen, and they come in a satisfying diversity. Some of them are hard to tell apart, but you don't need to catch them, or use a magnifying glass and a collecting box, or kill them and use a microscope. Birds come in great variety, but not an overwhelming variety. It is the sort of variety that you can cope with, whether you are a very good birdwatcher, or whether you are a very bad one.

Now, there is also another reason for studying birds.

They can *fly*. Have you thought for a second how amazing that is?

Flight is the dream of every human being. When we are lucky, we do, quite literally, dream about flying. Freud said that all flying dreams are really about sex. Perhaps they are: I've never found that to decrease their pleasure. They are the best of all dreams – you are free, you are miraculous.

The desire to fly is part of the condition of being human. That's why most of the non-confrontational sports are about flying, or at least the defiance of gravity. Gymnastics is about the power of the human body to fly unaided; so is the high jump and the long jump. The throwing events – discus, shot-put and hammer – are about making something else fly: a war on gravity.

Golf always seems to me a piffling game, but every one of its legion of addicts will tell you that it all comes back to the pure joy of a clean strike at the ball: making it defy gravity. Making it climb like a towering snipe. Making it soar like an eagle, at least in the mind of the striker as it reaches the top of its long, graceful parabola.

Think about it: all these sports are done for the joy of flying. Skating is a victory over friction, and it feels like victory over gravity; it feels like flying. Its antithesis is weight-lifting: a huge and brutal event, the idea of which is to beat gravity. All the horsey events come back to the idea of flight: of getting off the ground, of escaping human limitations by joining up with another species and finding flight. For every rider, every horse is Pegasus.

And birds, as you may well have noticed, fly. They fly in all kinds of ways: the brisk purpose of a sparrow, the airy insouciance of the seagull, the dramatic power of the hawk. Some birds specialise in flying very fast; others in flying very slow. Great hunters like the barn owl work on the edge of the stall all the time. Kestrels are very good at flying without moving at all. Some birds are not so great at flying. Pheasants just about get off the ground into a safe place in a tree for a night. They are poor fliers, but they are unquestionably better than us humans.

And flight attracts our eyes, lifts our heart with joy and envy. Flight, to us earthbound creatures, is a form of magic – one of the great powers attributed to decent wizards and witches throughout history is the ability to fly, from the persecuted sorcerers of the dark ages to the players of the game of quidditch.

And so we look to birds for a very deep-seated kind of joy. It goes back to the dawn of humankind: ever since humans first walked upright, they were able to turn their eyes to the heavens and observe the birds. The birds have something we can never have. But merely by existing – by flying before us – they add to the daily joys of existence.

Emily Dickinson called hope "that thing with feathers". Birds are about hope.

Take a basic urban moment – a commute, a traffic jam, a train becalmed. A sigh, a look away from the road or the newspaper, out of the window. A skein of geese in the sky; probably, almost certainly, "just" Canada geese. Too far away to hear them honking to each other, urgent instructions to keep the formation tight and to help the leader out with the hard work. A daily sight, a common sight, an ordinary sight. But just for one second – perhaps even two – you are let off the day's hassles. At least that is the case if you are a bad birdwatcher and you took the trouble to look up. It will probably be the most inspiring thing you will see all day. The day is better for those birds. You proceed with a smidgen more hope than you did before.

Birds seem – are – creatures apart. It is the convention of the west to draw the most sacred things with the feathered wings of a bird. Religious art is peopled with angels and archangels, epicene creatures with the wings of a swan. The Holy Spirit descends in the form of a dove.

Birds are, indeed, another class of beings. Quite literally: we are hairless apes who come from the class of Mammalia; they are feathered legions who fill the class of Aves. But another reason why we turn to birds again and again and in such numbers is because we have more in common with them than we do with many of our fellow mammals.

True, we can't fly. But take a walk with a dog. What do you do on your walk? You look about you, and listen, and when you meet someone of the same species, someone you know, you speak. Make a noise, that is. When a dog goes for a walk, he goes straight into the undiscovered country of smell. He sniffs the floor, he sniffs lampposts, he sniffs turds, he sniffs everything. When he meets a member of the same species he sniffs him or her. Specifically, he sniffs bum and crotch – a politeness among dogs, but not humans.

What is he doing? What does he understand from this? What is it like, living in the land of smell? Try telling colour to the blind. Humans can smell a bit, but we smell in black and white. Dogs can understand the entire spectrum of smell: they smell the world in glorious Technicolor, and cannot understand our bafflement, still less our impatience, when they wish to remain for some considerable time at the site of a particularly fascinating bit of smell.

Try reading up on mammal behaviour. Most mammalian lives seem to centre around a fascination with urination and defecation. Dung enthrals them; piss pierces their souls. They use urine and droppings for understanding who they are, who has been here, who claims this place as his own, who is interested in sex. All mammalian life is there.

And it is understood through the nose. Sniff sniff: this tells me all I need to know about the age, sex, sexual availability, position in the dominance hierarchy and – like as not – the personal identity of the individual that dumped and sprayed here. I am Dog; my name is writ in urine.

Most mammals understand the universe, each other and themselves through the nose. If you were to write a novel for a dog, it would have to be written not in sound symbols, like the words you are reading now, but in smell symbols.

And it is all completely baffling to us apes. We smell, as it were, bloody awful. But we have damn good colour vision and pretty decent hearing. These are the senses we work through. Colour and sound are our way of communication: and they form the basis for our art – for what is a book but fossilised sound?

Birds also have great colour vision and, like us, they inhabit the world of sound. Mammals are not colourful, save for the curious exception of the mandrill's arse, but then we apes are better at colour than most of our fellow-mammals. Mammals are mostly blacky-brownyruddy-grey. But birds rejoice in colour.

They communicate in colour: the brightly coloured birds flaunt their gorgeousness because, for a bird, gorgeousness is unambiguously about sex. When they court each other, they show off their colourful bits.

And they sing. They sing to tell us who they are and where they are and what they are and how bloody marvellous they are. And we humans, who can only guess at the world of smell, can thrill to the song of a nightingale almost as if we were nightingales ourselves. It has been suggested that the song of a nightingale actually alters the state of the female nightingale's brain, quite literally as if it were a drug. John Keats wrote that on hearing a nightingale, it was "as though of hemlock I had drunk": a perfect example of human empathy with birds.

Keats would not have written the same poem after smelling a pile of dog-turds. Humans cannot empathise with dogs, with fellow-mammals, in that way. But unquestionably, we can empathise with birds, thrill at their appearance and at their song.

Like birds, we humans are creatures of eyes and ears: we both love colour and sound; and birds make colour of outrageous perfection and sounds of perfect beauty.

Of course, we turn to birds. When speaking to each other, in their languages of colour and song, they inadvertently speak to us. They include us. And we cannot help but respond – so long as we have some streak of life left in us.

a. **Great Tit**
b. **Blue Tit**
c. **Coal Tit**

4. Let's fill the whole screen with tits

'From so simple a beginning endless forms most beautiful and most wonderful have been, and are being, evolved.
Charles Darwin, *The Origin of Species*

Let's start with the bird-feeder, for that is the easiest place in the world to get close to a bird, and it is the place where an awful lot of bad birdwatchers do an awful lot of their birdwatching. Many never get beyond the quiet and deeply pleasurable observation of the comings and goings of the garden and its ever-alluring tube of peanuts.

Which is fair enough, though you'd have missed out on my hobby had you restricted yourself to these limits. But right now, let us look out of the window at the peanuts and enjoy the birds that come to visit. And, as the Hollywood producer famously said, let's fill the whole screen with tits.

For it is tits that are famous for peanuts. Their name, by the way, is short for titmouse, which is a mixture of the *mose*, the Old English name for these birds, and the Middle English tit, a term for any small creature. Wrens have been called "titty wrens", and in Devon, apparently, "titty todgers". Some birdwatchers call great tits "Dolly Partons", ho ho ho.

But back to the tits that eat your peanuts. The first thing a bad birdwatcher notices is that tits are terribly good at eating peanuts; especially the little chaps that hang upside down. The second thing you notice is that there are two different kinds of tits.

The little blue chaps are blue tits, and the bigger fellows are great tits. They are pretty easy to tell apart, especially as the big fellows have bright yellow fronts with a black stripe down the middle. Blue tits and great tits are similar in some ways, both being tits and both liking peanuts and both being bold enough to eat them in front of your window. And both being acrobatic enough to hang in there and get them out.

But they are clearly different. So we have two interesting things to concern us. The first is that the birds are very similar, and the second is that they are very different. A whole lot of the whole meaning of life is caught up in those two matters, and we'll have more on the meaning of life as we go on.

As you watch, you will notice that the big chaps can chase off the little chaps whenever they want to. Great tits have automatic precedence over blue tits. If a blue tit wants a peanut, it has to wait for a great-tit-free minute, and then fly in and be quick and skilful. And by good fortune, or good evolution, quick and skilful is exactly what blue tits are.

So you can tell these two species apart, after not a very long period of study. And you could go on and look for another kind of tit; which is a good idea. Or you could wonder why on earth there are two different kinds of very similar birds who both like peanuts; and that is another good idea.

They have more than peanuts in common. They both like decent-sized deciduous trees, and they both like to nest in a hollow in one of those deciduous trees. They are, then, in competition for life's essentials – food and accommodation. And as we see, the bigger bird can always beat up the smaller bird. So how does the blue tit survive?

If you watch your feeder for a while, you will see that the great tit doesn't actually have to do any beating up. All it has to do is be there, and the blue tit will leave without even thinking of taking the great tit on. And if the blue tit is ever so slightly cheeky – or desperate – and looks as if he might want to make an issue of it, all the great tit needs to do is flex his wings – making himself look even greater – and the blue tit will take the hint and fly away. Better to lose a nut than your life, after all.

So why are there blue tits and great tits in the same wood, or even in the same tree? Why don't the great tits chase the blue tits off? The answer is simple enough: because they are not – apart from when they are both on your bird-feeder – competing for the same thing. Certainly, both birds look for caterpillars, grown-up insects and spiders in the warm weather, and for seeds and plant matter in the cold.

But in the main, the blue tit prefers to forage in the higher part of the tree, and out along the outer edges of the branches, while the great tit prefers the lower part of the tree and the inner part of the branches. In other words the blue tit's smallness – a disadvantage on the feeder – is a positive advantage in everything else it does. It can look for food in tighter places, hang from thinner twigs, and, being small and nimble, it possesses greater acrobatic skills. It can nest in a hole far smaller than one that would suit a great tit, too.

In other words, the great tits and the blue tit have quite different ways of making a living – they inhabit a different ecological niche, as scientists say. So we have before us two different ways of making a living in a wood, and God, or evolution, or whatever you care to call the process, has come up with these two different species to live them. Their lives overlap, but they are different in just about everything they do.

And they look quite different. The birdwatcher can't confuse them – and, crucially, nor can the tit. A great tit male and blue tit female couldn't get together and make medium-sized bluish babies. The two species look different and live different: and that's the way that the processes of life work. Life works by making lots and lots of very different forms of life capable of living in lots and lots of different ways. Which is why there are lots and lots of different kinds of birds; which is why being a good bird-watcher is very difficult, and why being a bad birdwatcher is endlessly fascinating. After all, when you've finally got the difference between great tit and blue tit clear in your mind, there are another 10,000 or so species to go before you've sorted out all the species in the world.

I bring you this notion of the immensity not to fill you with horror and make you give up, but to fill you with won-der. Watching birds, however badly, is like looking at the sky at dusk on a frosty night: endless numbers of stars, endless mysteries, and, the more you look, the more you see. Some can put a name to every star in the heavens, others can name just one or two, some can't even do that; but the great celestial mystery inspires awe in all who raise their eyes upwards.

And, as you continue looking at your bird-feeder, you will notice that there is a third tit that comes to snaffle the odd peanut. Smaller even than the blue tit, less flashy, too, but with a natty white stripe down the back of its neck. It's a coal tit, coal for the black of its head. And yes, it gets hooshed off the peanuts by blue tits and great tits, so it has to be pretty sharp and precise when it goes for a nut, and pretty patient while it waits for the bigger lads to get out of the way.

Now, you ask: how does a bird smaller than a blue tit survive? If a great tit works the middle of the branches while a blue tit works on the edges, what place is left for a coal tit? If a blue tit can feed on the wobbly far reaches of the twigs, then there is nothing left for any other bird, however small.

The answer is that the coal tit doesn't try to compete with the blue tit. It prefers conifers. It's even more agile than the blue tit, and it works the crown of conifers with great acrobatic skill, using its neat little bill to find insects and seeds *between* the pineneedles. It is not competing with the other, bigger tits: it has its own niche. It's only when there is a free meal going at a bird table that the coal tit clashes with the rest.

So it is not all a battle out there. Nature is not red in beak and claw. It is just that the bird-feeder is so desirable that – particularly when food is short elsewhere – it is worth coming down and scrapping and hustling and waiting for. This highly desirable commodity provides us with a crash course on the way birds (like anything else that's living) break down into different species. But it doesn't show us why and how.

Of course, it's not only tits that come to the bird-feeder, but let us, for the moment, turn our eyes away from the finches and sparrows and nuthatches and the occasional glorious visitation of a great-spotted woodpecker. Let us concentrate on the tits.

And – oh dear. Have you noticed a fourth tit? You might well have done, for they come to some gardens and some feeders. Sombre, quieter than the other three, almost a tit in mufti. And it is possible that you have got ahead of me and bought a bird-book and looked him up and despaired.

Because this is either a marsh tit or a willow tit – and do you know what? You simply can't tell the difference between them. This is the most horrible shock. They are both pretty ordinary-looking birds: tits without any of the attractive bits of the great tit, the blue tit and the coal tit. It is just a basic tit: greyish sort of a back and a black cap. Apparently the willow tit has a slightly less shiny cap than a marsh tit. Oh really? Buggered if I can see it. And it has a pale wing panel, and that's not the easiest thing in the world to see, either. Really: you make an effort to like birds and right at the start, they throw a curve ball like that at you. It's the rank ingratitude of it all that gets to you.

The only thing for a bad birdwatcher to do at this sensitive stage of development is to ignore it, in the most tactful way possible. Acknowledge the presence of the marsh or willow tit, but don't let it upset you. The point is that even so early in birding life, you meet an unfathomable mystery. And if we are not here for unfathomable mysteries, then what is the point of life?

Goldfinches

5. A present from my father

"What's yon bird, Romany?"

G Bramwell Evans, *Out With Romany Again*

"Make the boy interested in natural history." This was the last message from Captain Robert Falcon Scott – Scott of the Antarctic – to his wife.

It worked. The boy in question grew up to be a naturalist, a conservationist and one of my great boyhood heroes, Peter Scott. He presented the television prog-ramme *Look*. He also founded the Wildfowl and Wetland Trust, established its headquarters at Slimbridge, and was knighted.

"Every one should have a cause," he once said, or

allegedly said. "Even if it's only bloody ducks."

Alas, I have been unable to establish the authenticity of this excellent line, and when I tried, his widow had no recollection of his saying such a thing. Me, I like to think that the great wildlife campaigner was also a man who kept all the ironies intact.

That last request of the doomed captain always rather haunted my father. He was always keen himself. As a boy, he had once written to Romany about the early sighting of a celandine. Romany presented a natural history programme for children on what was then the wireless – my father still refers to the medium as "the wah-liss". Romany – at least the radio and literary character – was, obviously enough, a gypsy. He lived in a caravan, always referred to as "the vardo", he could speak Romany, he roamed from place to place about the countryside, and knew the birds and the beasts as old friends.

My father's letter was read out: little Edward Barnes of Wigan had indeed seen that delightfully and unexpectedly early celandine, had indeed found a little sun fallen to earth, there beside by his tramping little feet. This was one of the significant experiences of my father's life. He went on to work in children's television (as opposed to children's wah-liss), helping to establish *Blue Peter* as a programme in which the audience (like little Edward Barnes) actively participates, before going on to become head of BBC Children's Programmes, inventing *Newsround*, *Grange Hill*, *Record Breakers*, and Saturday morning children's telly. But he remained very keen on natural history, especially birds, though he never really had much of a clue what to do about it. Along with all those telly programmes, he also – at least, so far as I was concerned – invented being a bad birdwatcher. For me, it was the most important invention of them all.

Natural history mattered to him, and he was keen that I took it up. Like Captain Scott, he wanted to make the boy interested in natural history. In a way – like all fathers – he wanted me to do stuff he had never got round to doing himself. He wanted me to take his somewhat chaotic liking for wildlife and do something with it.

He gave me *The Observer's Book of Birds*, at the time the only identification book easily available. I read it from cover to cover, many times; I had it almost by heart. Cormorant, I read. Notes: an occasional harsh croak. I read all the Romany books, at his recommendation. I got them from the library, and I longed to walk through the country with the all-knowing, all-seeing Romany, and live in the vardo, and pull the ears of the spaniel called Raq, a dog Romany always spoke to in Romany: "Ava kai, Raq! Custa juckul!"

We lived in Streatham, in the heart of south London, and there was wildlife all around. I watched *Look* and I watched everything that David Attenborough presented. I realised before the age of ten that Attenborough was a genius, and for my school prize, when I left Sunnyhill School, I was given *Zoo Quest for a Dragon*, a book I still possess. My father, being a BBC colleague, got the great man to autograph it, one of the few autographs I have ever solicited, let alone kept.

I collected cigarette cards, and got all 50 Tropical Birds – I still remember the thrill of spotting number 35, the very last one I needed, the Indian darter. It was pinned to a notice-board in the staffroom at Sunnyhill School, and casting aside all shame, I begged for it. With an indulgent smile at the folly of small boys, the teacher, very decently, gave it to me. I wonder if he had any notion that birds would be a pleasure all my life, and, by the time I have finished this, it will be five books, including a novel, that I have written about wildlife and conservation. This shows the importance of a good education; and good education is all about the right cigarette card at the right time. Or the right bird, perhaps.

The Indian darter has a neck that looks like a snake, and it inspired plenty of wonder on its own, as well as doing its job of completing my set. I never thought that I would see real Indian darters, but I have – many times.

I was a member of the RSPB's Young Ornithologists Club. I wore the osprey badge, and read the magazine when it came. I thrilled above all to the story of the avocet. This was a bird that had gone extinct in this country. Extinct: that was a wonderful, heavy, doom-laden word. It thrilled me with despair on those days. The word has the same power to today: a word that lands on the palate and on the page with a dull thud. The avocet – dead as dodo, dead as dinosaur. But a miracle occurred: the avocet came back.

It was a story of incredible romance. This very odd, very singular looking bird, infinitely dainty with its eccentric, turny-uppy beak, had returned to us. It was incredibly rare, incredibly elusive, a secret, the sort of creature that normal mortals are not fit to see. I remember the huge surge of admiration and envy I felt when I met a man who had actually seen an avocet. I, however, held out no such hopes: seeing avocets was not for the likes of me. It was wonderful enough to know that the avocet lived again and bred anew; wonderful to be part of the secret and to rejoice. It was like knowing the location of a family of unicorns.

Now you will have noticed a flaw in all this boyhood

birding. There isn't much about seeing actual birds. The fact of the matter was that my father liked birds very much and wanted me to enjoy them, but he was a bad bird-watcher. Furthermore, he was a bad birdwatcher who didn't know how to be a bad birdwatcher. He didn't know what the next step was: he didn't know how you went from liking birds to enjoying them more fully.

He didn't own a pair of binoculars, and nor did I. Binoculars seemed far, far beyond me, like wanting to take a trip to outer space. I wonder now why this was so. Money was tight enough, certainly, but determined asking and scraping and saving would surely have won me a pair in the end. But somehow, I just didn't see myself as a person who owned binoculars.

So we were restricted to naked-eye sightings, which can be pleasant enough, God knows, but that way, you always keep the birds at a distance. Binoculars make the differ-ence: they bridge the gap between you and the birds. Above all, binoculars give you intimacy: the delight of being able to observe without being observed – without forever seeing birds flying away from you, uttering alarm calls. Perhaps naked-eye birding would be the best possible training, in the company of a skilled and enthusiastic observer. My father had only enthusiasm.

I remember one time he took me out birdwatching. It

was a sad day. We couldn't find any birds. We had driven, more or less at random, into the country, and we marched about on farm tracks on the edge of fields hoping to see a bird. All we saw was the odd little grey blob whizzing from one tree to another. It was the wrong place, the wrong time, we hadn't got the right equipment, we were short of knowledge.

"I don't think we're doing it properly," I said to my father, deeply wounding him. He responded with fury: "I spent days at a time doing exactly this when I was a boy." No doubt he had, but farming and the countryside had changed beyond all measure since those days. Neither of us knew that, then; very few people did. I remember we saw one thing and identified it. "Goldfinch," my father said, venomously pointing at the jaunty little chaps. He was right, too; I saw them quite clearly. They flew off, uttering alarm calls. It was the last birdwatching trip we made together for 30 years.

But I remember the sighting of a fabulous rarity. We – all the family – were on a boat, cruising up the Fal estuary, on what was ironically termed a pleasure trip. We had already spent several hours at sea. Some of the lads had spent their time trying to catch mackerel; I had spent my own time trying not to throw up. I have never cared much for boats, but, in the less lumpy water of the estuary, I recovered the will to love.

That last word was a typing error, of course, but I haven't got the heart to change it. Because there, high above the dramatic landscape, was a pair of burly birds, ragged-winged, gliding and soaring with insolent grace.

Buzzard. I could hardly believe I was privileged to be breathing the same air as so exceptional, so wild a pair of creatures. Perhaps you who read these words might smile at the idea of a buzzard being a rarity: in the West Country you see them all the time, sometimes 50-odd together. But back in the early 60s, buzzards were going the way of the avocet, the dodo and the dinosaur. It was something to do with the changes in farming, and it was a thing no one properly understood. It was a poisoning of the land unprecedented in history; and then, to see a buzzard was something deeply special. I have never forgotten it; I can still see them now, remember the impossible, nonchalant confidence with which they rode the big air. I think it was my father who first spotted them, though it might have been the boat captain or some other pleasure-tripper. No matter; I'll give my father the credit now. He deserves it all right.

But, without binoculars, you are pretty limited. You can never get intimate with a bird, never appreciate the detail.

Old naturalists solved the problems by shooting them: the great bird artist John James Audubon killed birds on a massive scale in order to produce one of the masterpieces of natural history.

But these days, we can most of us afford a pair of binoculars. Get a pair. It's the next stage in being a bad birdwatcher. Yes – but what sort should you buy? Ah, shut-up – any old pair, cheapest you can find, don't worry about it, don't think about the need for an investment. These days you can get crappy binoculars for no money, or not very much, and they may not be quite as good as the ones that cost getting on for a thousand quid, but they all have one thing in common: they bring the birds closer. It's not something to debate about. Grab anything; it's the start of getting intimate.

Birdwatchers are famous for being boring. I would reject that claim myself – birdwatchers are capable of having conversations that are meaningless to outsiders, but so are football fans, musicians and gardeners. But, when it comes to the subject of binoculars, I have to concede the point. Birdwatchers can be the most crashing bores on the subject of optical glass.

I have done it myself: well, I must disagree, I find the added weight a bit of a disadvantage, certainly but when you compare the size of image, etc etc, shut up and look at a bird. Birdwatchers are not boring about birds, but God are they – we – boring about bins. Never mind, I've got not one but two jolly nice pairs of binoculars, so aren't I lucky?

And if you haven't got any at all, get a pair now. If you think that there is the slightest danger of being able to increase your enjoyment of birds, then get hold of any pair of binoculars you can. And start looking through them. Ever seen an upside-down blue tit on a nut-feeder close up? Then it's time you did.

But as a boy, I didn't do that. This meant that my enthusiasm for birds didn't have enough to feed on. I grew up, or at least got older, and met a girl and went travelling and that sort of thing.

I always had a great liking for birds. I can remember the delight in the kingfishers when I went to Kashmir. I spent an hour counting the successful and unsuccessful dives one of them made from the stays of my houseboat. It was as confiding a bird as an English robin – no need for binoculars to get intimate with this chap, and he was successful far more often than you'd have thought possible. And I recall my fascination with the black kites when I went to live in Hongkong. I had a deep attraction to birds – and especially the idea of birds. But I didn't really know how to get to grips with the reality.

But I had a pair of binoculars by then. I had bought them for going to the races – to see the horses. And that made all the difference.

~~Willow~~ Marsh Tit ?

6. Teeming hordes

"O stop, stop," cried the Mole in ecstasies: "This is too much."

Kenneth Grahame, *The Wind in the Willows*

Perhaps you've already got a bird-book. That is to say, a book that seriously tries to help you tell one bird from another. It's called a field guide. Probably because no person who fancies himself a good birdwatcher would be seen dead carrying one in the field. It's a snobbery thing; you are supposed to know most of the birds already, and, if you can't put a name to one, you take extensive field notes (distinct supercilium, paleish edge to tertiaries) and look it up in your comprehensive collection of the best field guides when you get home. Eventually, you come to a thoughtful and mature conclusion and write it up at length in your diary.

Well, respect to all good birders who really do their birdwatching in this way – and yah-boo sucks to all snobs who never carry a field guide and hope that someone else will clear up the mystery, while they don't give themselves away too badly ("Ah yes, I see what you mean, and the longer primaries is diagnostic, isn't it?").

But what most bad birdwatchers do is have a thumb through while looking at the pictures and say: why, that's the chap. I'd know him anywhere. Which is all very well for a start but, as a technique, it runs out of steam after a while.

But we can worry about that later. The first thing to do is to get a field guide, if you haven't got one. Which one? The smaller the area it covers, the better. If you can get a field guide devoted entirely to the birds in your back garden, it would be ideal for starters. Unfortunately, most publications have a bit more ambition than that. My advice would be to cut out anything that bears the word "Europe" or, worse still, "North Africa". You can get some wonderful little books with perfect little drawings of all the birds you are likely to see – but they throw in things like wall-creeper, which you might see if you are dead lucky on a serious birding expedition to the Alps. Or Ural owl, which is helpful indeed if you happen to find yourself in the Urals, but a mite distracting if you are not completely sure of the difference between a tawny owl and a barn owl.

So try and get something restricted to the birds of Britain. You don't need to start your birdwatching life by confusing a curlew with a glossy ibis, or wondering why you didn't see a Dalmatian pelican (disappointingly, not a pelican covered in spots) on Margate Sands. But get a field guide. Any field guide. Thumb through it. Familiarise yourself with its salient points. If you don't mind a fairly gross suggestion, keep it by the lav. After all, learning about birds is just a natural process.

And you will see a number of birds you know, like swan and robin, and a number of birds you half-know – lapwing and nuthatch, maybe – and a number of others you have heard of. And the thought will hit pretty soon: bloody hell, there's an awful lot of them.

Aha! That's the whole bloody point!

Most field guides follow roughly the same order, starting with grebes and ending up with buntings. And you get towards the back of the book and start turning the pages that describe the warblers. And you discover, horror upon horrors, that it's even worse than the marsh tit/willow tit business. Your field guide might have 20 or so different species of warbler. If it is wider in its geographical scope, it might well have as many as 50. Fifty different birds – practically all of which look almost exactly the same. This is calculated to put off the most intrepid beginner.

These warblers look almost exactly the same in drawings that have been carefully produced and organised to show off their differences. Imagine how these birds are going to look when all you see of them is a fleeting glimpse of a browny-olivey shape flitting through the undergrowth. That's the trouble with birds: they very rarely stand still while you count their feathers and thumb through your field guide.

And you get resentful. What business have these birds, in being so ludicrously numerous? Why are there so many different species? What's the point, other than to confuse people who want to become bad birdwatchers? It's inconsiderate, it's off-putting, it really shouldn't be allowed. Perhaps the scientists are completely wrong and that this whole lots-of-different-species business is a fantasy, a work-for-the-sake-of-work scenario, something that doesn't matter in the slightest, something that is as pointless as counting the angels who dance on the head of a pin. It matters to the birds, though. A willow warbler may look almost identical to a chiffchaff, but it certainly doesn't want to mate with a chiffchaff. You are a human being. Imagine mating with a chimpanzee. The very thought is horrific: really profoundly disturbing. But humans and chimpanzees have 98.6 per cent of their genes in common. That is actually *more* than is the case with a willow warbler and a chiffchaff. A willow warbler, therefore, finds the idea of mating with a chiffchaff even more repellent than you find the idea of making love to a chimpanzee.

The question of species really matters, then, especially to the species involved. It is not something man-made, or imposed, a matter of pedantic irrelevancies. It is deeply and seriously real.

LBJs, say some people, meaning Little Brown Jobs. If life is too short to stuff a mushroom, life is certainly too short to try and tell a willow warbler from a chiffchaff, not to mention a Cetti's warbler from a Blyth's reed warbler.

Fair enough: stick to telling the difference between a swan and a duck when you start off. Don't let the bewildering variety put you off. Instead, let it inspire you. Bewildering variety is not an unfortunate occurrence. Bewildering variety is what life is all about. When you try to tell the difference between a willow warbler and a chiffchaff, you are not just posing yourself a puzzle to test your own observational skills. You are also entering into life's deepest mystery. The name of that mystery is biodiversity.

Every field guide that was ever printed is not merely a book of helpful hints on how to tell one bird from another. It is also a hymn to biodiversity: a song of praise for the fact that such a wonderful variety of creatures exists and has its being in our country, on our continent, on our planet. That line about "endless forms most beautiful", already quoted, is the last line of *The Origin of Species*, and every field guide will tell you about an awful lot of forms most beautiful, and, if the beauty dazzles and the endlessness of the forms boggles, stick with it. You are, after all, on your way to understanding the meaning of life, and that's not supposed to be easy.

Biodiversity is a bit of a buzzword, and it has become for many an eyes-glaze-over word. It means, at bottom, the fact that there are lots and lots of species. But it is more than that. Biodiversity is not just variety; it is also the fundamental strategy adopted by life on earth. For diversity is rather more than a conundrum for the observer. It is nothing less than the way life works. Life doesn't work by trying to make one perfect species. It works by making lots and lots of different species, each one talented at making a living in its own particular way.

There is a myth about evolution: that evolution is a

search for perfection. It is one of humankind's great self-glorifying misunderstandings, for guess which species always seems to embody that perfection – the paragon of animals, noble in reason, infinite in faculty? Yes, the whole point of evolution is you and me. Vast suns whirling through space, spinning planets, the collisions of asteroids, the primordial soup, the rise and fall of the dinosaurs: all of it was planned and preordained in order to produce me, writing a book about birds, and you, looking through the window at the nut-feeder and wondering why the blood doesn't rush to the head of the blue tit as he hangs upside down on the feeder.

That is the myth. But there is a real story of evolution which is much grander, much bigger, wider and higher: and infinitely more glorious. No one can say that a man is better than an arctic tern – a bird that spends every northern hemisphere summer in the arctic and every southern hemisphere summer in the Antarctic, commuting the entire length of the globe to live a life of almost perpetual sunshine. What human could do that? Or want to?

No: evolution – life – isn't looking for perfection; it is looking for survival, and life has come up with uncountable millions of survival plans. Each species has a different plan, and they all work. The summit of evolution is the arctic tern, or the woodlouse, or the blue whale, or the brown rat.

I used to think that scientists opened a bottle of champagne every time they discovered a species that was "unknown to science". If they did that, they'd be drunk from morning to night. How many species of animals are there alive in the world right now? Er, don't know. There are new species being discovered all the time, and each pushing back of the frontiers of knowledge only shows the vastness of our ignorance. Well, all right then. How many have we actually discovered so far? Er, don't know. There's no central list; that's not how science works.

But one tentative count, from the great scientist and thinker Edward Wilson, comes up with a number of 1,032,000, Of these, only 4,000, including ourselves, are mammals, with another 10,000 or so birds and a further 28,000 other backboned animals. There are 12,000 different species of nematode worms. A cake diagram shows that almost three-quarters of all living animal species are arthropods: that is to say, animals with jointed appendages and usually an external skeleton. Most of these are insects. That includes 98,000 flies, 112,000 butterflies and moths, and a whopping 290,000 beetles. That prodigious number gave rise to one of the most famous throwaway lines in the history of science. J.B.S. Haldane, another great scientist, was asked by his theological colleagues what, after a life-long study of creatures, he could assume about their creator. He replied: "An inordinate fondness for beetles."

Human beings come in one species, beetles in more than a quarter-million. Beetles are a quarter of a million times better than us. Quite clearly, the point of evolution is beetles. Other scientists will state that we live not in the age of man, but in the age of bacteria, and that the world has been passing through this age ever since the processes of life first began.

While we are on the subject of beetles, let us take a brief look at collection mania. Some people spend their life chasing rare birds and building a prodigious list of the numbers they have seen. I have already written a little disparagingly about the twitchers, and I will do so again later on. But twitching can, if you like, be understood as an act of prayer towards the concept of biodiversity.

For the greatest scientist that ever drew breath was a twitcher. Not a bird twitcher, but a beetle twitcher. His name was Charles Darwin and he was a maniac. His beetle collection was the driving force of his life when he was a young man, before he set sail on the *Beagle* to make an infinitely richer series of collections. There is a famous story about the callow and youthful Darwin scrabbling in an attic for beetles. He managed to capture two beetles unknown to him, and had one in each hand. But then he found a third. What would you have done? Darwin popped one of the beetles into his mouth and, with his now free hand, collected the third. This was the man whose book changed forever the way that human beings understand themselves and their place in the world. And it all began with twitching.

Watching birds is one way of understanding this revolution in thought. Understanding that evolution is not a tree with a bottom, a middle and a top, but a bush with a million twigs. Every twig is equally valid, equally important. Every different kind of bird we see is one of those twigs; every bird is another solution to the problem of life.

And in diversity, in the million solutions to the problem of staying alive, we find life. The meaning of life is life, and it comes in a million forms. And, if you wish, you can devote your leisure hours to the study of nematode worms, and good luck to you if that's the way life moves you. But birds are out there, the other side of the window, singing their hearts out and flying on their angel wings. When we turn to study life, birds thrust themselves upon us, with a beauty we can see and hear: and in a diversity that is staggering, but nonetheless graspable. Easier than beetles, anyway.

So you read the field guide and the ducks, right near the front, are full of charm and obvious diversity. You probably know a mallard, and a maybe a tufted duck or tufty. And that dapper little teal looks rather special, too; no trouble telling him from a tufty. But always there is lurking at the back of the book that terrible collection of LBJ's, that inordinate number of warblers.

There is a story about an expert birdman, the alpha male of a bird-ringing group, who caught a warbler. Surrounded by his disciples, he weighed it, measured it, rung it (ringers prefer the strong verb) and recorded all the details. It was, he said, with utter confidence, a willow warbler. He then let the bird go. Unabashed by its experience, it flew to the top of a nearby tree and sang: "Chiff-chaff-chiff-chaff".

And if an expert holding the bird in his hand can make a mistake, what chance have you got? Little enough. It's true that willow warblers and chiffchaffs have different leg colours – a chiffchaff has blackish legs; a willow warbler pale brown. But that can be pretty hard to see, since both birds like to lurk about behind plenty of leaves. And what's far worse, the leg colour varies. Birds are not only members of a species; they are also individuals. Leg colour is not something you can utterly depend on with willow warblers and chiffchaffs. But that doesn't stop them being completely different birds. Both species come to this country for the spring and summer, and spend the rest of their time in warmer places. But the chiffchaff goes no further than southern Europe and north Africa; some of them even hang around for the winter in Britain. But a willow warbler flies all the way to southern Africa. Imagine that – you could hold half-a dozen in your cupped hands; and they fly across the Sahara, and back. I have heard them in the Kalahari, singing the sweet song that you normally hear when the high spring is with us back home in Britain.

For you can tell them apart when they sing. That happens to be dead easy: the chiffchaff sings his name, but the willow warbler sings a lovely lisping trickle of descending notes. And I hope that, in time, you will hear it too.

But for now, diversity is the thing to cling on to. We are here to celebrate diversity. That is what birdwatching means, and it wouldn't be interesting if it was easy. So for now, the thing to do is to note that warblers exist, and do so in prodigious numbers, and then to concentrate on the easy birds. You are not bound to put a name to every bird you see. Nobody, not even the best birdwatcher in the world, can do that, so why should you?

A bird you don't know is not a mark of personal failure, a strong hint that you should give up, that the whole business of being a bad birdwatcher is pointless. It is just another small celebration of biodiversity; part of your own celebration of life. It was Einstein who said that the universe is not only weirder than we understand. It is weirder than we are capable of understanding.

SongThrush X 2

7. Falling in love again

That's right, the Mascara Snake – fast and bulbous.
Captain Beefheart

It is remarkable how much of our lives we spend doing things we really don't want to do. More remarkable still is how much time we spend doing stuff we think we are enjoying, only to realise later on that it wasn't enjoyable at all, and that we'd far sooner have been doing something else.

I feel these things very strongly when I look back at The Wasted Years: the years when I wasn't birdwatching, or even getting *The Observer's Book of Birds* by heart. I read books at school, all the time, and that wasn't a waste of time at all. But I did things like playing football, which secretly bored me, and getting involved in drama, which I secretly hated. When I reached the sixth form I was interested in revolutionary politics, for which I secretly had no taste whatsoever, still less talent or understanding.

Perhaps if the right opportunity, the right person had come along, I'd have been off a-birding. But perhaps not: I wished to be – needed to be – both successively and simultaneously – a good mate, a fancy-Dan intellectual and a dangerous radical. Birdwatching can cater for all those desires – I will demonstrate later on how hanging out peanuts for your blue tits is an act of revolution. But I didn't realise that at the time.

Then there was travelling and going to university and that sort of thing. I was involved in the traditional pursuits of youth, of course. But again, looking back, I secretly hated an awful lot of rock and roll and I was secretly terrified of drugs. The other part was all right, though no doubt an understanding of the way birds do it – in song and dance and finery – would have helped me on my way with my callow courtships.

This was the end of the 60s, the start of the 70s, and it was considered a fine, even enviable thing to be "into nature". Or better still "heavily into nature". A fine thing, so long as you didn't get too specific. "Wow, man! Far out!" That was the OK response to a sunset, a tree in the acid green of spring or the flight of a seagull. I think it's a pretty good response, on the whole, and I still think it when I see a barn owl, say, or I hear the first willow warbler of spring. Sometimes I even say it; it slips out in moments of unexpected delight. But then no birdwatcher, however good, however bad, ever really grows out of the wow-response. You just get to add other things to it.

But being too specific would have been a bit of a faux pas in those days. One of the set texts of hippydom – a book I never cared for – was *Jonathan Livingstone Seagull*. Jonathan Livingstone black-headed gull? Audouin's gull? Bonaparte's gull? Don't be uncool, man: it's a seagull, just dig it. Precision was frowned upon. "Perfect speed is being there," said the book. Or perhaps it was a glaucous gull.

There was a period in which I listened to the dawn chorus every day, though not entirely on purpose. I did it by staying up for it, rather than getting up for it. I well remember the daily horror of drawing back the curtains and finding instead of night a pale blue-grey morning alight with the cacophony of birds. "Hey, wow, man it's the tweeties! That's too heavy."

We compared the sound unfavourably to that of Captain Beefheart playing the saxophone. If you have ever heard Captain Beefheart playing the saxophone, you will understand that the tweeties were not soothing. It was a violent invasion, the new day interrupting our night, a great shock to the senses and to the mind. Odd, now, to think that I can listen to the dawn chorus – blindfold if you wish – and know most of the birds that sing. I can tell a thrush from a blackbird, and even, when the wind is southerly, a blackcap from a garden warbler. Had I been able to do such a thing then, I would have done better to keep quiet about it. Just listen and say wow. Not such bad advice, as I say. But you can add other things to it, which is what happened to me and why I am writing this book. The more you know, the more you wow.

After university, I started work on local papers and my principal memory of the first couple of years is of anxiety and stress and the feeling that I was never going to get anywhere. It was a horribly uncomfortable time, and no birds to help me through. These days, out on assignment, in the stresses and the self-pity that come from high-octane work, I almost always manage to slip away and spend a couple of hours birdwatching. I am a sportswriter by profession, but I have never been monomaniacal about sport, or anything else for that matter. A healthy biodiversity of interest is something to cultivate, I think. I remember, for example, a roseate spoonbill seen in front of a garbage incinerator in Tampa, when I was there covering the Super Bowl. It sent me back to the football with a spring in my step and a little calmness in my brain.

Birds are great removers of stress – so long as you are not a twitcher. A twitcher might be defined as someone who actively seeks stress in birdwatching. The very name came about because of the neurotic behaviour on view when these people are close to a rarity and believe they might miss it. But, for most of us, birdwatching works the other way: making life both richer and calmer, a pretty good double, I think you will agree.

So, I had no birds to help me with the stresses of the first years in a professional life. Just the memory of the pleasure I had once found in birds – or at least in the idea of birds. That and the occasional more-than-casual glance at such chance-countered delights as a kestrel hovering by the motorway, or a bunch of jackdaws riding a Ferris wheel of air in a winter wind. I had a hankering for birds, a nostalgia for birds. I just needed the right moment, the right excuse, the right place, the right person, the right bird.

Meanwhile, my father continued his high-profile, high-stress stuff at the BBC. He didn't do any birdwatching either. He looked at them all right, especially when he was on holiday in Cornwall. He, too, was waiting for the right place, the right person, the right bird.

I was unable to supply such things for him, nor he to me. The years of radical politics hadn't brought out the best in either of us. My father, for some reason, saw it all as a rejection of himself and everything he had worked for. He was unable to take things with a detached, boys-will-be-anarcho-syndicalists sort of air. And I had a wicked way of winding him up. The word "bourgeois" would do it every time. Never failed. Television was bourgeois, wearing a suit was bourgeois, drinking wine was bourgeois – not that this ever stopped me from enjoying my fair share.

We were not altogether reconciled during the university years. If I had dropped the political labelling and posturing, I was still intolerant of what we called "straight society". This too he took as a rejection. Partly it was, but the 60s were more than a Freudian rebellion-for-the-sake-of-rebellion. No. We all felt we were on the verge of creating a new way of living: more tolerant, less stressful, more spiritual, more meaningful – richer and more amusing. The accepted routes to this desirable state were the smoking of plenty of dope, wearing a great deal of fancy clobber, and an awful lot of music. The aims had a lot going for them; the routes were flawed. I have since discovered a far more effective way of getting closer to all those desired things. If you're still reading, you might guess what it is.

But please remember that there was, in the full outpouring of hippydom, a deep and heartfelt desire to put things right. There was a feeling everywhere that things had gone badly amiss in modern Western life: and that it was our job – our duty, our destiny – to make it better. Or at least to do our best. Perhaps you think I should have grown out of all that sort of thing. I have not. I still feel that there are one or two areas in which Western society has got it a bit wrong; I still feel that we should do our best to make it better. I don't think I am unique in this, either.

And quite a lot of all this comes down to birdwatching; it really does. Birds are not only a delight; they are a cause, a battle, a purpose, a meaning – and no trivial one either. I will be talking more about that later on. But before the meaning comes the joy. Marriage, for many is what gives life its meaning. And in marriage, before the meaning comes the joy. You don't find the meaningfulness of marriage without first falling in love. I want every reader who likes birds – who, as it were, *fancies* birds – to move on. Stop ogling them from afar and make your big move. Stop admiring birds; start falling in love with them.

The 60s had substance behind the poses, you see, though the posing seemed pretty important at the time.

Naturally, this involved a fair amount of perversity. Take Tim. I was to meet him a few years later, and he was to teach me a huge number of birdwatching skills and, more importantly, pleasures. He was so perverse that he not only refused to wear a tie. He refused to wear a shirt as well. But birdwatching with Shirtless Tim opened my eyes.

My father obviously approved of my getting a job after university – he had been half-expecting me to decamp to India and never be seen again. Amazing to think that had I gone, I would have done so without the guidance of Salim Ali, the doyen of Indian ornithology and creator of India's first field guides. I once saw a shikra – a jet-propelled Asian hawk – when covering a cricket match in Bangalore, but that is by the way.

But I wanted to write for my living, and journalism offered the only obvious option. So with a suit and a tie, and hair at least a little trimmed, I set off to work for the *Surrey Mirror* in Redhill. One of the first stories I did was about somebody who had a pet owl – a tawny, as I recall. It shat on my suit. As if to say: "Bourgeois!"

I remember talking to my father during the worst of my time on local papers, bullied, oppressed and persecuted by an editor who admitted later, "Of all the journalists I have had under me, he was the one I hated the most." I groaned and told my father about the horrors of having to go to work the following morning. He said: "I have never not enjoyed going to work." There was still a gap in understanding, then. I felt oppressed by the scale of his achievement and his total absorption with his professional life; he felt bewildered and disappointed by my poor showing and my lack of relish for the great world of jobs.

Well, I did go to India. I went as part of my annual leave, not as a drop-out. Though I was, naturally, seeking the meaning of life. And I loved India from the first moment. How could anybody not? My heart was filled with the East after that: and I had to go and live in Asia. A couple of years later, I was living on Lamma island, a 45-minute ferry ride from Central District, Hongkong, working as a freelance journalist, travelling all the time to various thrilling places around the region. And seeing the occasional thrilling bird. I was never quite sure whether my ignorance was part of the pleasure. I loved the mystery of the great birds I knew nothing about, but there was something inside me that wanted to put a name to it. Obscurely, I felt that the name mattered.

Lamma has or had a good few nice birds – it's been built up hugely since my time. In particular, there is the bird that nobody ever sees. In spring, it sings a four-note call, again and again: the first and third notes the same, the second note a semitone lower, the last with a drop of a minor third. So a musician told me, anyway. When the spring ran hot and strong in the blood, and the moon was high and the wooded slopes and the maniacally manicured market gardens were washed in silver light, the Chinese cuckoo sang all night. "One more bot-tle! One more bot-tle!" If ever a bird sang the national anthem of a place, it was the Chinese cuckoo. In those boozy days at the far end of the Empire's tether, it was advice we seldom rejected.

I didn't know it was a Chinese cuckoo then, of course. But when a friend of mine – another lost birdwatcher who never watched birds – told me it was a Chinese cuckoo, I was quietly satisfied. Obscurely, I felt it mattered. Obscurely, I felt that the meaning of things, the ability to put a name to things, was important. And obscurely I wanted to put a name on even more things. I didn't know how, of course, but I had a feeling that it was important.

yellowHammer

8. Simon knows the names of things

And Adam gave names to all the cattle, and to the
fowls of the air, and to every beast of the field.

Genesis 2.20

Jeremy was, and no doubt still is, a raffish and rather fastidious intellectual. He made his living by translating French novels into English, and he used to play for Tewin Irregulars, a raffish and not-at-all fastidious cricket team I helped to run. Jeremy was an elegant and immensely reliable right-hand bat – reliable insofar as he practically always turned out for us. He was less reliable when it came to the scoring of runs, but he always looked good. Shirtless

Tim, incidentally, used to play for the Irregulars as well, bowling speculative medium-pace.

Jeremy had no interest in birds. Literature, exotic girlfriends and an establishment in Clapham called The Tea-Room des Artistes fulfilled most of his needs. And he once sent me a poem. It was called "Simon knows the names of things". He told me that he awoke one morning with this unexpected sentence running through his mind, and the only way to get rid of it was to turn it into a poem. It is a nice sentence: rhythmic and ringing with those four Ns, and it was a nice poem.

But it is the last line that has stayed with me. I like it, I think, though I am still not quite sure whether or not to take offence. Does it mean that I am wise and widely learned, a person people to turn to whenever they find a void in their knowledge? Or does it mean I am a nerd, someone packed with useless information that no one wants to know about, a person always imparting facts more interesting to myself than to others? In short, something of a full-time bore? Well, since this was a nice poem, the answer is probably both.

But it's true. I do know the names of things. Some things, anyway. I like words and names and I have a mind that tends to hold on to them. I have, for example, been gazing at a pebble identification chart. It came free with a magazine and it has been on my desk for some days, and I keep looking at it in obscure delight. I knew what a flint was, but did you know what a chert is? Well, flints and cherts are both kinds of silica, or quartz pebbles. A chert has a typically waxy lustre. The illustration is beautiful and shiny, and it looks as if I could pick it up from the page and chuck it across the room. It looks like a pebble: and every time I see a pebble just like it, I shall say: Ah, observe the waxy lustre. This is a chert.

Do you know what a schist is? Did you know that the pink pebbles that look like little fossilised brains are in fact flints cracked and coloured by fire? Do you realise that this little chart could change my relationship with pebbles for ever?

Because names matter. Names of everything. You feel noticeably different about Jane than you do about that woman from accounts. If you go regularly to a nice pub, the landlord and landlady will not only learn your name, but they will make sure that you know theirs. They know that the learning of names changes your relationship with the people and thus with the pub. If you fly business class, you find the staff are trained to call you by your name: a small ploy to make sure you feel you are getting your money's worth. Another whisky, Mr Barnes? The poor sods at the back just get sirred.

I have given myself considerable quiet pleasure in recent years by trying to learn butterflies. I have done it extremely badly. If I am bad birdwatcher, then I am a perfectly appalling butterfly-watcher. I'm barely at the nut-feeder stage. I know only the common ones that I see around where I live: peacocks, small tortoiseshells, meadow browns, and so forth. But never mind – life is richer even for this poor fund of knowledge. Knowing some of the names makes me look at butterflies in a way I never used to: I like to see who it is that has come a-calling. I look more, I see more, I relish more. Sometimes the painted ladies come, and even I know that they come here on migration, flying over the channel on their silly, feeble, fluttery wings, and when I see a few – they generally arrive mob-handed – I can savour the small miracle of their arrival. In Cornwall last summer, the cliffs were swarming with clouded yellows. Before I learned my poor few butterfly names I would scarcely have noticed them. As it was, they added pleasure to every day.

I am even worse at trees. I love to be with people who can tell me their names, so that I feel that small but significant change of relationship that comes from knowing a name. I learned to recognise field maple, for the excellent reason that I had some planted in a hedge. Now I can recognise it when it as part of ancient hedgerow. I walk past an ancient hedgerow every day with my dog. You can tell that the hedgerow is ancient because of the mix of species. A friend of mine explained that, and told me some of the names. I liked the hedge well enough before, but knowing these few things about it makes it better. This scrap of knowledge adds to its mysteries rather than taking away from them. There is a particularly chunky field maple up by the stile. I know its name, it has shared something with me.

My understanding of the tree, the butterfly and the pebble has altered in some curious way because I know their names. That is because knowing something's name is a highly significant thing. It is the most significant thing you can tell someone about yourself. An American will announce his name with his first breath; the English prefer to keep people waiting before imparting that treasured scrap of information.

And what, after all was Adam's first job? It was to name all the animals. Naming comes first; everything else follows, including Eve. Adam had to establish some kind of understanding of the world he lived in and the creatures he shared it with. So naturally, the first task was the naming of names.

It seems clear that Adam was history's first bad fowls-of-the-air-watcher. It is also the fact that bad birdwatching makes Adams of us all. Birdwatching is a way of changing your relationship with the world, and it begins with names. You might argue that humans gave the creatures their names, and that a yellowhammer won't care one way or the other whether your call him a yellowhammer or a Cretszchmar's bunting or, for that matter, a Dalmatian pelican.

But a yellowhammer is still a yellowhammer. A yellowhammer knows it's a yellowhammer even if he doesn't think of it in those precise terms. The cock bird knows he is a bird that sings "a little bit of bread and no cheese", and the hen bird knows the cock has a bright yellow head. And it's no good either of them being vague about the subject of being a yellowhammer, because they can't make babies with a Cretszchmar's bunting, still less a Dalmatian pelican. And, if you are not out there doing all you can to become an ancestor, then what is the point of being out there at all? In evolutionary terms – and how else does life work? – none at all. It matters to a yellowhammer that it is a yellowhammer: and it matters to a yellowhammer that he and she can only make little yellowhammers with the help of another yellowhammer. A female Cretszchmar's bunting simply won't make a male yellowhammer go "phwoar". And calling him a yellowhammer is our human way of recognising this important fact (of course it's important, ask the yellowhammer). And with recognition comes the beginning of understanding. If you like, the beginning of science.

Science is the study of names. Science names everything: processes and things, living and unborn. Everything starts with a name. Philosophers argue about the importance of a name. A name demonstrates the existence of a shared concept; yellowhammer is not one person's wacky idea, it is a bird we can all know and have a relationship with. There is no such thing as a private language: in order for sounds to become a language, they must be shared. A name is the sharing of a thing. And by acquiring the name, you can share it with me, with everybody who likes wild things. I can tell you that I saw a nice bird the other day, and you can say, ah yes, good. But I can tell you that I saw a yellowhammer, and you might almost have been with me.

I have talked a lot here about the change in relationship that happens with the acquisition of a name. Naturally, this is a one-way relationship. Let's not get all silly and new-age-ish about this. Birdwatching is almost by definition a one-way relationship: you try very hard not to disturb the bird. You don't want it to fly off. You don't want it to know you are there; you don't want it to know you exist. It is considered very poor show to bung a brick at a ringed plover to make it fly off so you can see whether or not it has wing-bars (if it hasn't, it is a little ringed plover, and *much* more exciting). One of the great treats of watching nature is to do so when the creature observed is completely unaware of your existence. It is a very special joy; more, it is a very special privilege, and I have done this with elephants and rhinoceroses as well as with yellowhammers.

A one-way relationship is very far from an invalid one. I have, for example, a very important and – to me – very meaningful relationship with James Joyce. True, he died before I was born. Joyce doesn't know I exist any more than that yellowhammer does, but both, in their different ways, are important to me.

But then I deal with one-way relationships all the time. I write about sport and people frequently have extremely intense relationships with the people who do it. People who watch sport have significant feelings for David Beckham, Steve Redgrave, Jonny Wilkinson, Sir Alex Ferguson, Paula Radcliffe, Venus and Serena Williams. Only one or two of these, so far as I know, is aware that I exist. (I have been told that Ferguson once referred to me as "fucking Simon Barnes". I am planning to adopt this as a byline.)

Thus the plunge of a little tern into a coastal pool, or the sudden impossible blue shimmer of a whizzing kingfisher does not mean that my sudden flight of joy is shared with the plunging or shimmering bird. But it is joy nonetheless. And it is joyful particularly because when I see the flash, I don't have to wonder what it is. I am a good enough bad birdwatcher—or at last an experienced enough bad birdwatcher – to see the blue flash and to be able to put a name to that flash. Kingfisher!, I say, where another might say, bloody hell, it couldn't have been, could it? And mine is the heart that leaps.

Avocet

9. Alice's key

And she ran with all speed back to the little door; but alas! the little door was shut again and the little key was lying on the glass table as before, "and things are worse than ever," thought the poor child.

Lewis Carroll, *Alice's Adventures in Wonderland*

Once you start to look at birds – once your eyes follow the flight of a passing crow or a bunch of starlings whirling across the road without any conscious decision having been made – then sooner or later you will have a sight of such wonder and perfection that you will always be a bird-watcher. This is nothing less than a statistical certainty. It is a sight, a moment that confirms your growing interest and makes it part of your life for ever afterwards. It is the moment when you realise that birdwatching isn't something to do with other people. You, too, can see wonders.

It might be a great spotted woodpecker coming to the nut-feeder: something so marvellous that you feel astonished to be sharing the same planet. It doesn't worry you that great spotted woodpeckers are pretty common birds, and that seeing them is a knack relatively easily acquired. When you see the picture of them in the field guide, they look outrageous: impossible that so extraordinary, so gaudy a bird should exist in this country, still less flaunt itself before you.

Suddenly you have the key to those wonders. Poor Alice wanted to get into the beautiful garden, but the key was on a glass table and she was too small to climb its slithery legs. "How she longed to get out of that dark hall and wander about among those beds of bright flowers and those cool fountains." Then she grew enormous and she could reach the key all right, but she was now far too big to get through the door. All she could do was lie on the floor and put her eye to the door and peer at the gorgeousness that was forever out of reach.

This is a sad tale about the horrors of growing up, and the sense of wonder that you leave behind you when you become big. For me, birdwatching became Alice's key: birdwatching opens the door to the garden. But this sight of wonder, this conversion experience, this confirmation bird, does something that Alice's key never could. It makes you small enough to enter the door. There is something childlike about the best of birdwatching: the sensation of seeing wonders – and it gives endless savour to the more grown-up aspects of the pleasure, the naming and understanding and relishing.

When I lived in Hongkong I fancied myself as a bit of a wheeler-dealer, like everybody else in that town in those days. I was asked to write a series of travel pieces for an in-flight magazine, and was offered a decent sum of money for doing so. Not good enough. I said I would do it in exchange for two return tickets to Sri Lanka, to be donated by the airline I was writing for. After a bit of arguing, they agreed. I wrote nine city-portraits (The striking contrast of ancient and modern at the busy hub of Asia's teeming metropolis, etc, etc) and collected two economy class (so I just got sirred) tickets to Sri Lanka. The second ticket I gave to a girl named Cindy. The selection of that name is probably the only unkind thing her mother ever did in her life, but that was and is her name, so that's what I call her.

We spent six weeks on that wonderful island and

did everything: beaches, ruins, temples, towns, villages, elephants. We made a supposedly risky trip to Jaffna, the Tamil area, shortly after the library had been torched by the police, so that I could get a story for the Far East *Economic Review*. It was a great trip: and it had one significant omission. I had not visited any of the wildlife parks.

I didn't want to go. I resisted. I had a horror of doing it badly, of being disappointed. I had a hunger to see wildlife, but a desperate need not to be caught up in some unsatisfactory experience. In short, I was afraid.

It was the last day of our trip. We had a flight that afternoon. We were in a town called Hikkaduwa, which was then a hippified beach resort where you could get an avocado milk-shake and a pair of drawstring trousers with buttoned ankle cuffs. And Cind went off for a bit of shopping, and went vague. She came back after two hours with a seraphic smile on her face and some nice presents for her family. So we missed the plane. There wasn't another plane for a week. And because my ticket was a freebie, it couldn't be transferred to another airline. We were stranded in Sri Lanka. There are worse things that can happen to a chap, especially when he is accompanied by Cind. I knew I should be back in Hongkong writing up some of my stories, but we had a plan and I was intoxicated by its beauty. It was Cind's plan: a plan that cut through my own nervousness. I was nervous because I wanted, quite desperately, for things to go well.

We were going to devote seven days to wildlife. We would go to as many wildlife parks as we could. I would write about it, naturally. And we would do it properly. I managed to hire a pair of binoculars in Colombo – the idea of travelling without binoculars seems to me absurd, as if this story took place not so much at another time as to another person. But anyway, shared binoculars at our side, we set off.

And saw instant wonders. The first park was Gal Oya, a drowned forest with semi-submerged trees full of heraldic cormorants. We travelled by boat, and had distance glimpse of elephant, and absurdly wonderful water-birds. We were doing it properly, it seemed to me. And we were both enthralled. But that was not my conversion experience.

The following day, at a place whose name I have forgotten, we found ourselves walking across mudflats with a guide, following the dried soup-tureen footprints of an elephant. We never caught up with him, but the pursuit was stirring enough. And then, a long way distant, I noticed some birds. Rather dainty birds, long-legged wading birds, with thinnish beaks. In an unaccustomed movement, but one that would soon be a part of me, I raised my hired binoculars to my eyes. And entered heaven.

Avocet.

I was incapable of speech. The mythical bird of my childhood, the bird that had come back from extinction, the bird that had gone and had miraculously returned, the bird that no one was permitted ever to see – there it was in front of me. A group of about a dozen, gorgeous in their black and white, sweeping their dainty-upcurved bills through the water with a scything action. I felt like the shepherds as they gazed on the flight of angels.

From that moment, I was a bad birdwatcher. I have never looked back.

And so I invite every beginning bad birdwatcher to step outside in search of the conversion experience, the confirmation bird. I do so in the absolute certainty that it is out there waiting for you. And that is it wonderful, and will always be with you.

How do you find it? Just look. Look, and seek to name. And the easiest way to see birds is to go out and walk. As with everything to do with wildlife, you should set out with high hopes and low expectations. You should be ready to be sidetracked, and, above all, to revel in what you see rather than what you want to see. I once made a trip to hunt for tiger and never saw them. But I had a wonderful trip-making sighting of the Ganges dolphin, three of them to be precise, leaping out of the water: white and blind, living in the murk and silt of the Ganges river system and finding their prey and each other by sonar, like dolphins from outer space. It was worth travelling for that moment, and my father, who happened to be with me, agreed. But more of that later.

The most popular activity in Britain is going for a walk in the country, and it's about the best, too. The country being also the park and the common and all the urban local spaces. And here's how you do it. You put one foot after another, and when you see a bird, you stop, and put your binoculars to your eyes and say: "What the bloody hell's *that*?"

You can improve your skills, but the technique I have just described is perfectly acceptable for starters; and it's good enough to serve you for the rest of your life. The rest is only refinement.

And you learn what the bloody hell they are by thumbing optimistically through your field guide, looking at the pictures until you say: Ah! Here's the chap. And all at once you find a very good reason for having a field guide that covers as small an area of country as possible. A quick skim through a more ambitious work, and you are totally convinced that you have seen a black-headed bunting. Sorry, but it wasn't. I know. Trust me. You have to go to Southeast Europe and Asia Minor to see a black-headed bunting. What you saw was a reed bunting, and very nice too.

It's not very scientific, this thumbing-through technique, but it's the way to get familiar not just with species of birds but with the larger matter of family. It helps, for example, if you know that the bird you saw was an owl. That narrows is down to the five species you are likely to see in Britain, so you are almost home already.

If you see a bird you have never seen before, but you do know another bird that is quite like it, then you can start looking at birds on nearby pages. All thrushes have pretty much the same sort of shape, and if it's not one of the ones you know about, like a mistle thrush, song thrush or blackbird, then it's probably a near relation. And there it is, on the next page: a fieldfare, and you saw a bunch of them on an open field in winter and got a half-decent view of the black tail.

You start by blundering about and making a good few blunders, too. Everybody does. My advice is to carry on blundering in a totally unembarrassed way. The more you look, the more blunders you will make, and the more blunders you make, the more you will see, and you find that slowly that a pattern has been building up without you realising it. This building-up of patterns is one of the deeper joys: once you begin to understand the rhythm of birdwatching you are beginning to understand the rhythm of the birds themselves. Which is nothing less than the rhythm of life.

I got back to Hongkong with my mind ringing with avocets and all the other wonders I had seen in Sri Lanka, and the first thing I did was to buy a bird book: after *The Observer's Book of Birds*, the best bird book of my life. It was called, appropriately enough, *A Colour Guide to Hongkong Birds* and it was packed full of wonderful drawing by Karen Philips, and a plain, helpful test by Clive Viney. Hongkong is small: not all that many birds, not all that many places. It was a great place to start and the right sized book to start with. It included useful local information such as the fact that the black-necked starling is frequently seen on Fanling golf course and that you will see azure-winged magpies in the Botanical Gardens.

And by dint of walking and looking and thumbing through the book, I soon learned the more obvious local birds on Lamma island, where I lived. I already had a pair of binoculars, the ones I got for horse-racing. They cost HK$100, or about ten quid; not a lot, even then. They were, in snobbish birdwatching terms, or even in ordinary optical terms, complete crap. But even the crappiest binoculars are great. My binoculars were utterly brilliant. They brought the birds closer, you see.

One of the first things I realised was that the rock on the edge of the harbour was the favourite fishing perch of a kingfisher. Crowds of people, hundreds at a time, marched past within 20 feet, to and from the ferry eight times a day, all indulging in cacophonous Hongkong conversation; and the kingfisher sat there, bobbing his head and occasionally arrowing into the chill waters to come up with a tiddler. It had, presumably, always been there. But I was a bad birdwatcher now. I saw him every day.

The great thing about being a beginner is that it doesn't take much to please you. And if you have any sense, you will keep that. But the initial naming of the common birds – literally the common or garden birds – is a great voyage of adventure, as well as the basis of something that you will give you joy everywhere and always.

I have brought the *Colour Guide* to my desk for reference as I sit writing these words, and just thumbing through the book, as of old, looking at Karen Phillips's gorgeous illustrations, takes me back to that time when a magpie-robin at first filled me with the thrill of discovery, and then with the greater joy of familiarity. I saw him – jaunty, black and white, bold and confiding as an English robin – and I knew his name. It was a new intimacy: with the bird, with my beloved island, with all of nature.

But there were gaps, too. Pages and pages I didn't really want to look at: two pages of warblers, a page of pipits. I only ever saw a couple of the warblers, though Clive Viney assured me that plenty of them were common enough. And the pipits and larks all looked the same. I hurried past those pages, slightly embarrassed at my ignorance, but also secretly doubting that these birds really existed, and whether or not it mattered. I was opening my eyes, which was great. But that was only a start.

Bittern

10. Well done, medium or rare?

Aye, madam, it is common.
Hamlet

We value what is rare. We can't help it: twenty pound notes are rarer than pennies, beautiful girls are rarer than plain ones, diamonds are rarer than flints or, for that matter, cherts. This brings us to the question of rare birds. And it is one of those strange facts of life that there are more common birds than rare ones.

There is a popular notion that all birdwatching, whether done by good or bad birdwatchers, is about rare birds. The reason for looking closely at a flock of sparrows

is to see if there is some bird of indescribable rarity –
perhaps a first winter savannah sparrow – lurking half-
concealed among his less glamorous pals. If there isn't, you
let the sparrows go and cast your eye elsewhere.

Well, what is a rare bird? You can look at the idea
entirely from your own viewpoint, and say that a rare
bird is any bird you haven't seen, which is fair enough,
if limited. Or you can say that a rare bird is any bird
that nobody sees very often. Perhaps a barn owl, a bird
that eluded me for some years... but I now live in
a place that barn owls like, and I see them very often, so
in a single bound, barn owls have gone from rare birds
to – well, not exactly common birds, but certainly birds
that are part of the routine of life. So barn owls aren't
rare in any demanding sense of the term.

Or what about the laughing gull? You won't find that
in your British field guide. But a laughing gull was
seen at St Mary's on the Scilly Isles in November 2003,
according to what is thrillingly referred to as "an
unchecked report". This is a very rare bird indeed, and it
will have given great pleasure and excitement to those that
saw it, and they will have no doubt spent subsequent
months waiting in agony for the checking of their report. I
was not among those that saw the laughing gull. And I
have seen heaps and heaps of laughing gulls: I have visited

a brackish lagoon that was thronged with laughing gulls filling the air with their laughter. The sound is described in one field guide – for these birds do appear in field guides, you just have to get the right one – as *ha-ha-ha-ha-ha-haah-haah-haah* etc, which about covers it.

Now ask yourself why I have seen flocks and flocks of laughing gulls, when the sighting of a laughing gull is a matter of great excitement to such august publications as *British Birds*. Perhaps you leap to the conclusion that I must have been lying all along and that I am in fact an extremely good birdwatcher. Not so, alas. So perhaps the answer is that I know of a secret place where these birds are to be found.

Got it in one. And that secret place is North America and the West Indies. I remember the brackish lagoon from Antigua; I was there for the cricket tour in which the West Indian captain, Viv Richards, failed to get onto the pitch in time for the start of the match because he was in the press-box slagging off a journalist. Every evening when work was done for the day, I would sneak off to the lagoon and take a stroll, enjoying the walk, the birds, the laughter.

Laughing gulls are common on the far side of the Atlantic, and they are exquisitely rare here. That is because they don't live over here. They live over there. You might wonder what that lone laugher was doing on the Scilly Isles. So, I imagine, did the gull. He didn't mean to be there at all. He had got lost: blown across by unsympathetic winds.

You can walk through Central Park in New York in the autumn, and, as you fight off the muggers and endeavour not to snag your feet on too many syringes, you can see any number of small American warblers: yellow-rumped warbler, American redstart, ovenbird – lovely little birds. Common birds, true, but well worth seeing. Every year, a few of these get blown across the Atlantic, and some of them get spotted by eagle-eyed good birdwatchers. But what happens to the birds?

They change in an instant from being very common birds to being very rare ones. And then, mostly, they die. They are not equipped to make a living here. They are in the wrong country, and exhausted by a ludicrous journey they never wanted to make. No wonder the people who seek them get twitchy: they have to get there in time to tick the bird before the bloody thing keels over and dies.

That is how things work at the extreme end of the rarity business. And there are more and more rarities turning up; or, to put it another way, more and more being noticed. Birdwatchers not only have access to all kinds of information that wasn't readily available in former times, but most of them travel abroad to look for birds, which was impossible for normal people 50 years back. These birdwatching travellers will have seen laughing gulls by the hundred in North America or the West Indies; and are therefore able to spot a doomed wanderer with relative ease.

Of course, they don't all die. There was once a black-browed albatross that somehow ended up in the wrong hemisphere and fell in with a bunch of Northern seabirds, and travelled with them on their annual commute to winter feeding waters and summer breeding grounds. He was to be seen for years, for albatrosses are long-lived creatures, off the coast of Scotland every summer, a bird greeted annually with great affection and called, obviously enough, Albert, which is short for albatross.

These windblown vagrants are rare if you think of them as British birds, but generally, they are not at all rare in global terms. You can read about them, most particularly in *British Birds*, and they are treated with scientific language and a passionless fastidiousness. Which is fair enough, though the recording of lost birds doesn't seem to me a scientific pursuit of the highest possible value.

Let's go back to that flock of sparrows, the one in which the first winter savannah sparrow lurked so memorably. A rare-birds-man would leap at the oddity, the rarity, the freak. But a true ornithologist would be more interested in the sparrows. For here's a thing: birdwatcher and ornithologist are by no means the same thing. A birdwatcher likes looking at birds, and may be very good or very bad. An ornithologist is a proper scientist. Perhaps he or she is preparing a paper on about mate selection in house sparrow *Passer domesticus*, or is conducting a survey on flocking dynamics, or perhaps this ornithologist is a conservation scientist on the cutting edge of the science and is researching the mysterious decline of the house sparrow. It is more important and interesting in scientific terms to know where the sparrows have gone, to suggest a way to arrest their decline and perhaps a method of bringing them back up to decent numbers, than to relish the thrill of the rogue savannah sparrow.

In fact, compared to stuff like conservation science, the pursuit of rarities looks decidedly thin. It is not science. It is not ornithology in the terms that someone who studies species-specific brood parasitism and mimicry among the indigo birds of southern Africa would recognise it. But it is something I recognise very well, being a sportswriter by trade. It is sport. In fact I once made this remark to Rob Hume. Rob, editor of the RSPB's *Birds* magazine, for whom I write every quarter, is not a bad birdwatcher. He is a birdwatcher a very long way beyond good; so good he was for a time chairman of the Rarities Committee. You can't really be a better birdwatcher than that, for this is the committee that sits in judgment on such solemn issues as first records for Britain. They examine all the evidence, most particularly your field notes, and after deep esoteric discussion they come up with a decision. Yes, they say, it *was* a red-eyed vireo. Or they say, well, I'm awfully sorry, but there is still an area of doubt here. And their judgment brings joy to some and anguish to others; for that is the way these things go. Some you win, some you lose.

Course it's not bloody science, I told Rob. It's bloody sport, innit? Rob laughed and said: "Well yes, obviously."

Bloody good sport it is, too, the addicts tell me. Good on 'em. Any way that people enjoy their birds without harming them seems to be a very good thing indeed. But chasing and collecting rare birds is not the only way to do birdwatching, it is not the whole point of birdwatching, it is not what the best birdwatchers do all the time.

I say this not to demean the rare-bird chasers, but to clarify things for the confused beginner. "Bit of a twitcher are you?" people will ask you, when you have come out of the closet as a bad birdwatcher. People think that bird-watcher and twitcher are synonyms, and that if you are a birdwatcher, you are chartering planes and hanging out with crowds of strange fellows, all of you hoping for a sight of that bobolink that was certainly there yesterday.

There are many other kinds of birdwatching, and I will tell you about them as we go on. In the meantime, I suggest we all stop worrying about rare birds of the Arctic redpoll and Northern parula kind. But perhaps I have confused you. I mentioned the names of a dozen or so mega-rarities and you say: Well, what about the birds in my field guide that I haven't seen? What about the avocet? What about that hobby you went on about back in the first chapter?

Well, no, an avocet is not a rare bird, not when compared to a semi-palmated sandpiper. If I wanted to go and hunt for one, I would only have to leave my desk for an hour or so. It's not a rare bird, not like those American and Siberian wanderers. Let us just call it a special bird.

A bittern is a special bird. It's not rare like that bobolink. In late April and early May, I know exactly where to go to find one; nor is that knowledge a secret. But there aren't very many of them. They are rare because they make their living only in wet reedbeds. They are not very adaptable. They are specialists: they are brilliant at working with reedbeds, but they struggle in any other kind of habitat. Such specialisation is something that people working in the science of extinction call "the tender trap". Bitterns may be great at wet reedbeds; but if you take the reedbeds away, they are buggered. Their specialisation –

their very brilliance – has undone them.

And reedbeds have indeed been taken away at a ferocious rate, mainly with the draining of land for agricultural use. Bitterns were common as sparrows before the draining of the fens. But these days, rivers are controlled and canalised. Reedbeds are no longer forming spontaneously. These days, bitterns are rare because reedbeds are rare. No home, no bird.

If you are interested in looking after wild birds, then the bittern is much more important than the lesser yellowlegs that turned up in Northumberland. The lesser yellowlegs is rarer, but the bittern is a very great deal more special. It is more important, in the grand scheme of things, to look after the special birds than to merely clap eyes on the mega-rare ones.

Though clapping eyes on the special birds is one of the great special experiences of life. Dawn on Walberswick marshes in May, and one of the great concerts of a lifetime: nightingales hammering away from every side, giving out their impossibly loud and varied repertoire from the tree behind. And in front of us the bass boom of the bittern. I stood and listened for a good hour, because times this special don't come for the asking. And then, in that soft orange light of first sun, the bittern came out of cover – for they are birds far more often heard than seen – briefly paraded in his reed-coloured livery, and then withdrew into his kingdom beneath the seedheads.

Now that is birdwatching at its best: not the chasing of the rare but the untroubled contemplation of the special.

It's all in the way these things take you, of course, but it will do for me. Rarity for its own sake is not the point. In fact, I wish the bitterns were a lot less rare. Avocets were once extinct, and you can't get much rarer than that. Extinct as breeding birds in this country, anyway. And now if you go to the right place and you can see breeding avocets all over the place. Go to Minsmere in April, go to that great bird reserve in Suffolk, and you won't be able to bung a brick without hitting an avocet. In the right places avocets, once the rarest of the rare, are nothing less than common. And there is not a birdwatcher, good or bad, who believes that is anything other than a good thing.

So, as you come out of the closet as a bad birdwatcher, you can do so in the knowledge that there are special birds out there waiting for you to revel in them – and also in the knowledge that the pursuit of rare birds is nothing to do with you unless you want it to be. It is a specialised business, with a specialised language. It doesn't matter scientifically. It is not essential to chase rare birds if you want to be a birdwatcher. It is not the heart and soul of birdwatching. It is not even a question of lowering your sights; it is about choosing the manner in which you enjoy your birds.

Some of the very best field observers – very good birdwatchers indeed – never chase rarities. They are "local patch" people. Their satisfaction is their concentration on a single place, where they observe the comings and goings of the birds, day by day, season by season, year by year. Bad birdwatchers do this informally; very good birdwatchers do this in minute detail and keep lovingly detailed diaries. Many of them will observe and identify the occasional rarities and do so with glee, but it is bread-and-butter daily observation that enthrals. It is the best of soap operas.

In other words, some of the very best birdwatchers are more interested in common birds than rare ones. In fact, the notion of common birds and rare birds begins to look like nothing more than a kind of snobbery. Perhaps you thought that there was a hierarchy of birds that takes the birdwatcher on from the lowest of the low – those sparrows, perhaps – to the highest of the high: that first for Britain that is hurled into the country on the back of a howling gale from Siberia and is miraculously spotted by a hawk-eyed observer the second before the poor bird pegs it.

But that is not the case at all. Just before I wrote these words, I came in from a hard January frost and a feeble winter sun. The sun didn't do much for me, but it stirred the soul of a dunnock. A dunnock is perhaps the LBJ of all LBJs, the bullish, brownish, smallish, skulking little thing that is about as common as another of his names – hedge sparrow – might suggest. And he, ignoring the cold, was filled with a sudden excitement about the coming of the warmer weather. In that iron frost, he felt the tug of spring; and he sang his heart out as a result. It's not a great song, compared with that nightingale on Walberswick marshes. It's not a special bird, in terms of peak experiences; I'd come in telling everybody about my hobby, but I wouldn't take up anybody's time with a dunnock moment.

But there he was against the cold blue sky, every feather picked out by the low winter sun and he sang his song of spring and gave it absolutely everything. It was a song that made the whole day better. A common bird: a rare moment.

Smew

11. Shirtless Tim and a nice bit of posh

"See, O Bagheera, they never thank their teacher.
Not one small wolfling has ever come back to thank
old Baloo for his teachings."

Rudyard Kipling, *The Jungle Book*

My Father gave me a reward when I was able to do my tables, from once two is two all the way to twelve twelves are a hundred and forty-four. It was *A Field Guide to the Birds of Britain and Europe*, dated now but recognised as both a classic and a revolution in bird identification. How odd it was to be birdwatching with my bedraggled copy more than 20 years after I had acquired it by knowing that seven eights are fifty-six. Back from Hongkong, I had to set the divine Karen Phillips aside, and return to my old friend Roger Tory Peterson.

I visited odd places, and looked at birds, generally with Cindy, who was by then my wife, and we had fine times and muddled along and saw a few birds here and there. There was always a feeling of being in over our heads, but that was rather agreeable. We visited woods, parks, lakes, the Norfolk Broads. I had what you might call a second Confirmation Bird here. I had read about marsh harriers before, and knew them from The Young Ornithologists Club. I knew they were birds of fabulous rarity: only one or two birds nesting in Britain at secret locations.

And I saw one. They are unmistakable birds: nothing flies like a harrier. They cruise with wings held in a shallow vee – a dihedral, to use the nice technical term from aerodynamics, which I remembered from the cadet corps at school. And, as with my Sri Lankan avocets, there was that sense of amazement and privilege. I wanted to drop to my knees; I wanted to whoop with excitement; I wanted to weep for their scarcity and weep again because there were still here; here, now, in front of me, quartering a field in a remorseless dihedral, performing every now and then a shuttle-cock drop onto some luckless creature of the reeds.

I was not thrilled because it was a tick, because my list was at a stroke one bird longer. Birdwatching is not trainspotting, and must never be confused with such a thing. Birdwatching is – this harrier was – a soul-deep matter. It was more than beautiful; it was a meeting, and understanding, a linking of myself with the bird and the world. My heart in hiding stirred for a bird – the achieve of, the mastery of the thing!

If you think my prose style has suddenly changed for the better, I must sadden you. That last sentence is from Gerard Manley Hopkins. Idiot interviewers are always asking victorious sports stars: "How does it feel?" They reply: "I'm over the moon," or "It hasn't sunk in yet." When Hopkins saw his kestrel, for the poem I was quoting is for a kestrel rather than a harrier, he didn't have any one to ask him: "Father Hopkins, how did it feel when you saw that bird?" ("My son, it hasn't sunk in yet.") But he was to tell us anyway:

Brute beauty and valour and act, oh, air, pride, plume here
Buckle! And the fire that breaks from thee then a billion
Times told lovelier, more dangerous, O my chevalier!

All of which confirmed me as an English birdwatcher. I bought a pair of second-hand binoculars for 40 quid, and they weren't bad, ten times better than my hundred-buck racing jobs, anyway. I had come out of the closet as a bad birdwatcher in England: bins, field guide, sense of wonder, sense of both trespassing and belonging, and the habit of taking walks while carrying binoculars. That difficult transition phase from casual, naked-eye viewing to committed walking and binocular-carrying has been accomplished pretty comfortably. And I was ready to move on a stage further.

Which brings us back to Shirtless Tim and the mighty Tewin Irregulars. What a great cricket team we were. I kept wicket; it was generally agreed that the strongest part of my game was the shouting. Tim was one of our more regular players. It was proper cricket, no jeans-wearing pick-up game. We all wore proper gear: white trousers with a white shirt and white woolly in cold weather. Tim, of course, played in white trousers and a white tee-shirt. I don't recall any one ever remarking on this, apart from the time when he had got his laundry out of sync and played in a white tee-shirt emblazoned with a large aubergine.

It's a matey business, playing cricket, and there is plenty of time for talk. Not much, admittedly while waiting for your turn to bat, because of the ever-precarious nature of Tewin Irregulars batting, but at least in The

Plume of Feathers afterwards. And so we talked. Tim wrote, mainly novels for children. He is a person drawn to the north, the cold and the uncomfortable; the warm and the lush repels him. A tent, the farther edges of Scotland and its islands, Scandinavia: such are his pleasures. By no means puritanical, certainly not in his choice of post-match relaxation, he nevertheless has a certain gluttony for austerity.

He is hugely knowledgeable on an astonishing range of subjects, a great enthusiast for sport, for the children's books of C.S. Lewis, for combative conversation ("Not at all, Stalin was quite right..."), and for discussing Tewin Irregulars and their failures with a point and vividness. He is also a memorable giggler, which probably explains why his period as a schoolboy Maoist came to an end. He once clean bowled one of the best batsmen who played against us – a man, I believed, who played for Berkshire Second XI. (At village green cricket matches, there is always someone who used to play for somebody's second XI.) This paragon was homing in on a deeply resented century when Tim inadvertently bowled him a ball that soared skywards from his hand: the biggest, ripest and juiciest full toss ever seen, even at Tewin. The man from Berkshire Twos opened his shoulders to swat the ball away for six with a finely judged contempt. Alas, he missed. The ball landed on top of the stumps. Tim did not punch the air, or whoop, or cheer. He fell to his knees with helpless laughter.

A good companion, then, and not a man you meet every day. And a birdwatcher. Having established, over post-match pints, that we both cared for birds, it became inevitable, after having shared enough humiliations of the cricket field, that we should go birdwatching. It was pretty clear that Tim knew what he was talking about here, and that I did not. But Tim, with exquisite sympathy, never made an issue of this. He just led, picked the routes, showed me the birds, and acted as if I really knew as much as he did but was too shy to make this knowledge public.

I can't tell you how important this phone-a-friend business is, if you wish to go on to more rewarding ways of being a bad birdwatcher. If you have a friend who birdwatches, exploit him or her for all he or she is worth. For a thousand reasons, the friend is likely to be eager to come with you. It is a real pleasure to show people birds, it is real pleasure to share birds, and besides, it is an excuse to get out and do it when you would otherwise be creosoting the fence.

Tim took me birdwatching. He knew where to go and when to go: essential skills. He was familiar with certain places, and he knew what to look for in them. He was an experienced birdwatcher. He knew what he was likely to see, and what he was less likely (but hoped very much) to see.

We went first to Staines reservoir – an intimidating sheet of black water with a wind that sucks the warmth from your body and blasts the flesh from your fingers. I remember my momentary dismay: endless numbers of birds, sitting on the water, and not a single one I recognised. I was overwhelmed by panic. Tim put me at ease with consummate tact; all at once he started to recite a reassuring litany of the most obvious birds. And sanity returned; a pattern emerged; outcrops of knowledge appeared in a landscape of ignorance. Yes, of course, there were great-crested grebes, they just didn't have their great crests, it being winter.

Soon I was aware that Tim was able to recognise birds I could hardly see at all, a fractional glimpse, a dart, or a distant dot, and he would tell me the name of a species. Since Tim happens to be a bullshit-free zone – he abandoned bullshit long before he abandoned shirts – I knew he wasn't showing-off or making it up. It is customary on such occasions to remark on the acuity of vision thus displayed, but Tim has terrible eyesight. He wears glasses at all time, and, to see a bird, he has to nudge the glasses off his nose and jam the eyepieces of the binoculars over his newly denuded eye. (Most spectacle-wearers, incidentally, can use binoculars and spectacles together; Tim somehow never got the hang of it.)

So I couldn't say: "What good eyes you have." I was forced, instead, to say: "What a good brain you have," though I didn't say it out loud. But I rapidly became aware that Tim was able to process very scanty visual information in a meaningful way, and I was not. This was not because he saw better than I did, it was because he looked better. My sister Rachael lectures in art. She is better than I am at looking at paintings, because she has had a great deal more practice and has given it a great deal more of her mind. We don't really see the same painting at all: she sees her paintings in the context of a lifetime of acquired knowledge. As Rachel with pictures, so Tim with birds.

Much as I like looking at paintings, I like looking at birds still more. (I think they have more to tell us.) And like every angst-ridden teenager, I wanted to be better looking. Or least, better *at* looking.

Tim knew some old gravel works where cold weather would sometimes drive the delightfully natty little ducks called smew; and we found them, more than once – a bird I always associate with Tim. At one time, deep in his past, Tim had a girlfriend from one of the smarter parts of

Essex, insofar as these exist. She was, in fact, a nice bit of posh from Burnham on Crouch. Tim had come out of this affair a much wiser man: he knew exactly where you could find short-eared owl in winter.

And so we walked one whole and glorious and bitter winter day, from Bradwell nuclear power station to Burnham on Crouch, looking not for bits of posh but for short-eared owls. And all kinds of other stuff as well. For that is one of the constant pleasures of birdwatching: you never know what you will see. The usual stuff is usually there to enjoy, and, as for the more special things, they might come, or you might be thrilled by something totally unexpected and unlikely: the Ganges dolphin rule.

Thus Tim and I found red-backed shrike when hunting for smew, and white-winged black tern when hoping for black tern (which we got as well). But perhaps that walk towards Burnham on Crouch was our definitive expedition. For there, at least half-a-dozen times, we saw the not-at-all elusive short-eared owl, in plain view, there so that we might admire his cross expression as he squatted on the ground, or his marvellous, balanced, floppy-winged flight, poised forever on the edge of a stall. Tim was my Gandalf: a magician who could pull birds from the air, from the trees, from the ground, put a name to them, and change my relationship with them forever.

The walks came to an end when Tim moved to Dorset. I have scarcely seen him since those days, though I send him good vibes on a regular basis. Last time we talked, he spoke with the greatest distaste of birdwatchers and, by implication, birdwatching. They were all ignorant fools with overpriced optical glass who blundered around not knowing that they were looking at. These days, he only looked at invertebrates, and was particularly hot on butterflies and moths. A man not without perversity, as I have said.

But he showed me birds all right. There was nothing prissy about it. Nothing difficult, either. We didn't sit in a hide staring at nothing; we didn't stand for hours peering through a telescope. On the whole, we went for a walk, and we talked just about all the time: the time the Tewin Irregulars captain ran out four batsmen in a single over, the time that man from Berkshire seconds was out to Tim's full-bunger, the impossibility of any one ever taking over from Liverpool at the top of the tree of English football, Moby Dick and Aslan, girls from the past and from Burnham on Crouch. And birds, birds, birds: where to find them, how to know them, birds we have known, birds we have missed, birds we have shared, birds we have never forgotten. And we generally had a pint at lunch and another pint or two when we got back to town.

I was a bad birdwatcher still, but a much better one than before. Better, not so much in the extent of my knowledge as in the extent of my enjoyment. Tim lifted the limits I had set myself, and showed me things that lay far beyond. He turned what had been special birds into birds of daily delight, and he turned birds of mythology into birds of occasional and glorious reality.

As a boy I turned the pages of bird-books looking at birds I knew I would never see. Now I see birds I have seen and birds I may yet see. And by turning the birds of myth into birds of feather and blood, I have not taken away from them their sense of mystery. *Au contraire.*

Tim was a good birdwatcher, a bloody good birdwatcher, but not *that* good. His was not the sort of talent that was out of my reach; and he was always, with great generosity, sharing his knowledge, helping me to try and catch up with him. Not by instruction so much as by example. He shared some great and glorious birds with me - and did so as if it were the most natural thing in the world.

Long-tailed Tit

12. And all that jizz

One thing I know, that, whereas I was blind, now I see.

John 9:25

It's easier to cover England than any other football team. When I am writing about an England game for the *Times*, I know all the players. I know what they look like, I am familiar with the way they move. If I see someone with a fancy haircut playing a 50-yard ball from somewhere out on the right-hand side of a pitch, I know it is David Beckham. I don't have to see his number. If I see a stocky chap making a rapid, scuttling run up near the front, I know it's Michael Owen. I know the formation England play in, I know the habits of the individual players, I know their haircuts, I know the way they run, what kind of body-shapes they make. It's easy. It's less easy with club sides, though Manchester United are familiar enough and so are Arsenal. After that, it gets harder: I simply don't watch enough club football to have the knowledge. My colleague, Matt Dickinson, the *Times* football correspondent knows all the top clubs about as well if not better than I know England. It would be highly to his discredit if he did not. It is, after all, his job.

The other day, I had to go to Northampton to cover an FA Cup match. Yes, they were playing Manchester United. Now understand this: all the Northampton Town players looked different. They had different haircuts, different faces, different skin colours, different ways of moving, they were of disparate heights and diverging body shapes. To make things even easier to tell them apart, each helpfully wore a different number on his back. I had a team-sheet, football's equivalent of a field guide. The diagnostic feature of each player is his number; the sheet said which number applied to which man.

Despite this flawless information, I struggled to keep pace. I always do in such situations. In the hectic ebb and flow of a football match, you can't always see a player's number. You have to rely on other, less tangible things,

things that are not clear from the field guide. You see a player cut in from the left and cross under heavy pressure from a United player; you see the contrasting colour of his shirt, you know that the United man is Phil Neville, but the other fellow's already crossed and I have to look for the man trying to reach it, because if he scores, I need to know who he is, and it would have helped if I knew who had given him the cross, and I've already missed it.

Meanwhile, in front of me, there was a man who watches Northampton Town every week, and he knew the name of the cross-supplier. He could recognise him in the dark, knows that's what he does, how he moves, where he turns up. Matt, who had a seat on the opposite side of the ground, would certainly be doing better than me, because he is much better at watching football matches and understanding the patterns and the individuals who create them. But even he finds it harder to watch Northampton than England.

So why do I find it easier to watch England than Northampton? Well, I can recognise the players even when I don't see them properly. I know it's Beckham even when I can't see the number, the name, the haircut. I am deeply familiar with the look of him, with the cut of his jib. And if I see a little ginger fellow appear out of nowhere, I know it is Paul Scholes, and for the same reason. I have looked at both many, many times. I have a clear image of them in my brain, I can process all kinds of small and rather vague clues and they combine to give an immediate and totally accurate identification.

That is what birdwatchers call jizz. Jizz: savour the word. Jizz is a very good word indeed. It's a word of obscure origin, and not to be found the *Shorter Oxford*. Some have suggested that the word comes from an obscure dialect form of the word "guise". Others have speculated that it is a jovially flawed acronym (like OK for All Correct) – perhaps from the United States air force, and their need to be able to recognise enemy aircraft for General Impression of Shape and Size. Experienced etymologists will tell you that acronyms are almost always guesses. A friend of mine suggested that the word is a contraction of "just is". As in the answer to the question: "How do you know it's a lapwing?"

The wonderful book, *A Dictionary of Birds,* claims that the word was coined by a chap called T. A. Coward in 1922, and defines it as a "combination of characters which identify a living creature in the wild but which may not be distinguished individually". Rob Hume, former head of the rarities committee, wrote a book called *Birds By Character*, subtitled *A Field Guide to Jizz Identification*. "Lengthy country character", it says for magpie. "Canny, knowing every trick". Note the careful avoidance of scientific language, the flight from precision. Identification by jizz is by definition vague and hard to categorise. I talked to Rob about the etymology of jizz, and after we had spoken, he embarked on a Google search for the word as he sat at his desk at RSPB headquarters in Sandy. Alas, his screen was flooded with the most lurid types of porn, and he was forced to abandon his investigations before he got sacked.

But let's have another bash at explaining jizz. You get up in the middle of the night busting for a pee. It's not your own place, you have been royally entertained, and the thing to do is to get to the lav and back without waking the entire house. And God, it's difficult: hands in front of your face, doors at odd places, the corridor twice as long, or perhaps twice as short as you had supposed. You bash your hip on a table and jar your shoulder on the door, and the desired retreat that is your goal turns out to be down a step that certainly wasn't there when you went to bed. And then you have to get back – slightly easier, because you've learnt the route, but still tough enough.

Now let us say that the position is reversed. You are the host, you have royally entertained your guest, and once again, you need a midnight pee. You stroll along the corridor at your ease, and back again. You need no light, you take no false step. You see that small metallic gleam: it is a doorknob, it tells you exactly the position of the door, the angle at which it is open; that slightly paler oblong is your destination. You ascend the waiting three steps without ever having counted them in your life, and your hand is there at just the right height to find the door-handle.

In one house, you can see in the dark; in the other, you are blind. It is a striking contrast, and you had drunk just the same amount in each house. So what has happened?

Familiarity enables you to process scanty information and interpret it in a meaningful way. You may not be able to draw a foot-perfect map of your own house, but you can read those small clues and walk through the darkened corridors as easily as if it were midday. You can't tell it, but you most certainly know it.

That is the principle on which jizz works. Jizz is the art of seeing a bird badly and still knowing what it is. And there is only one way of learning how to do it and that is by watching birds. Not chasing them or ticking them. Watching. Birdwatching is a despised term in some circles, which prefer the meatier term "birding". But, without watching, there is no birding. You watch, you seek a name, you carry on watching, and from watching you learn. Or rather, you absorb. You see your bird from awkward angles, making curious, ungainly shapes, half-hidden by leaves; as we have already noted, birds do not, in the main, line up in profile looking hard left, as they always do in field guides. No field guide can teach movement; you can only learn it by watching. Silhouetted birds, flying across a field – that one with the all-day rowing action is a crow; that buoyant glide and side-slip is a gull. That switchbacking flight is a great-spotted woodpecker. That flap-flap-glide is a bird of prey.

Once you have begun to get the hang of jizz you have begun to get the hang of bad birdwatching, and good bird-watching too. Of course, jizz is never wholly infallible: a bad glimpse of a small white bum disappearing furtively into the bush could indeed be a bullfinch, as you thought, but it might also be a brambling. But looking and absorb-ing the shapes and sizes and movements – the general vibes of a bird – is how you begin to get the hang of the birds. You get to know them. You get familiar with them; they get to become part of your life, not just as birds, but as members of a species. From the chaos of biodiversity comes a pattern, and from the pattern comes the beginning of an understanding. In a strange way, the bird you have learnt becomes your friend; or, if your prefer, your relation. As indeed they are, being fellow-vertebrates.

You can recognise friends and relations in a way that

you can't recognise strangers. Rob, who wrote the jizz book, likes to compare jizz to waiting on King's Cross station. Say you ask me to meet your wife, husband, father, mother, son, daughter, at King's Cross. You send me a description you have written yourself. You send me a photograph. I make sure I learn both. And is that just the same as you doing the meeting?

It is not. You can recognise the person without reference to description or photograph. You can recognise any one of them from 100 yards through a crowd with their back to you. It is not just recognition; they are part of you. And that is what happens when you begin to get the hang of jizz: the bird becomes part of you.

You acquire the skill of jizz recognition simply by looking. By looking at birds you have already identified; because, you see, identification is the beginning and not the end of the process - and that is why birdwatching, good and bad, is the exact opposite of train-spotting. Every seeing is a moment of greater understanding. Every seeing makes the bird more fully a part of you, a part of your life.

And again, I don't mean this in a sloppy New Age way; I mean it in a hard, no-nonsense way. You can't recognise a bird by jizz unless it has become a part of your life: until, that is to say, its pattern and behaviour are stored in your brain, ready to be accessed next time you lay eyes on it.

You start with the common birds – how else could you do it? There are, as I have said, more common birds than rare ones. And understand this: the hunt for rare birds can't be done until you know the common ones. How do you know it's rare unless you know all the other birds that are not rare?

When I travel abroad to an unfamiliar place, I seek to learn the common birds. The ambient birds, the birds that are always around in towns and suburban gardens. Once I have got the more obvious birds under my belt, I can begin to understand the place where I find myself. I have some kind of grounding. And when you have cracked a dozen of the most common birds and you see something else, well, then you know it must be slightly more unusual than the birds you have already got the hang of. You have a place to start, even if it is a negative one.

Let's go back to this country. You see a little bird, and it has the jizz of a tit and yet it's not like any of the tits you know, and you know blue tit and great tit, coal tit too on a good day. And you are pretty certain it's a tit even if it is a bit pink and the shape isn't quite right. You know it's not a great tit or a blue tit because you know those birds by jizz. But something about the jizz of this new little bird is a bit tit-like. Or new little birds, because there was a crowd of them, being very busy and bustling and agile and acrobatic and tit-like in the upper branches of a tree in the park. So you know the first place to start looking is among the tits, and the first place not to look is great tit and blue tit and coal tit. And by golly there it is: long-tailed tit, and you always thought they were fabulously rare. "Unique, tiny, ball and stick shape," says Rob in his jizz book. And you watch them, and next time you see a group of bouncing, cheeping, pinkish ball-and-stick birds in a treetop you will say: "Aha! Long-tailed tits." And you won't have seen them at all well. You will have recognised them by their jizz.

It is like learning a foreign language. The first couple of phrases are obvious: *bonjour, je t'aime, pas du tout*. The next stage is hard, but once you have got a pattern and you can make sentences, you are away and talking. And even if your accuracy is at times suspect, you can normally make yourself understood. Bonjour, je suis un spectateur des oiseaux tres mechant.

Jizz is the key. Jizz is the beginning of understanding. Woody Allen famously described himself as being "at two with nature". Once you start recognising birds by jizz, you move away from that terrible duality in which we live; a world with humans on one side and everything else on the other. You begin to find some kind of unity; you begin to understand, not just with your mind but with your gut and your heart as well, that there are no hard and fast boundaries. You, a mammal, can reach out and have some kind of understanding of these feathered fellow-vertebrates. It is one of the most liberating feelings on earth.

The more you look, the more you see. Every passing minute is richer, more rewarding. The more birds you see, the more birds you see. When you recognise the patterns of daily life among the birds you know, you will recognise something that breaks that pattern. Those familiar starlings, feeding in a gang on the ground, quarrelling companionably with each other. And in an instant they are all gone: Why? What?

And you learn to look up when this happens, and behold. You are rewarded – a sparrowhawk swerving away, missed its pass, the starlings were too fly this time. Once you understand the ordinary, you prepare the way for the exceptional. Once you have begun to savour the quiet joys of everyday birds, you have made yourself ready for the peak experiences. You are ready for that combination of the gloriously normal and the staggeringly unexpected that is the heart of the life of the bad birdwatcher, and the good.

Followers of Zen have a saying: when the pupil is ready,

the teacher will come. When the birdwatcher is ready, the jizz will come. It comes slowly and cautiously, and it must be cultivated. It is not acquired consciously; it is just that the more lapwings you see in flight, the more you will recognise their floppy-winged passage through the air. Jizz: if you can let the birds come to you, the birds will stay with you.

Gadwall

13. Treasure houses

Hardly had we started when we came across signs
that there were indeed wonders awaiting us.

Arthur Conan Doyle, *The Lost World*

The best thing about Streatham was the 49 bus. It used to take me away from Streatham, away to the great Treasure House of the Natural History Museum. In those days before paedophiliophobia, I used to take the enchanted bus there every Saturday at the age of nine and ten, and gaze on stuffed birds, stuffed mammals and the bones of dinosaurs. That apart, Streatham didn't have much to recommend itself to a boy birdwatcher. Admittedly, Naomi

Campbell was born in Streatham, but too late for me. At any rate, there was no one like her at Immanuel Church youth club.

But, despite the obvious disadvantages, we lived there for years. It was not an address that suited a media mover-and-shaker like my father – perhaps that was one of the reasons why the "bourgeois" jibe was so effective. But it was a nice house, and my father, by means of trial and error and serious thought given over to labour-saving, had made the garden a very pleasant place for sitting and drinking. Streatham Common was a hundred yards away, and there he would go for a walk with Duff, an important part of his daily routine.

When the birdwatcher is ready, the birds will come. Two or three years after I had returned from Hongkong, my parents moved. My mother, by the way, wrote for television. She wrote one series about the museums, collections and stately homes of Britain. It was called "Treasure Houses".

By the time of the great move, my father and I were pretty matey. I had made a fair success of Hongkong, despite the somewhat unfortunate start of getting sacked within six weeks by the *South China Morning Post*. I managed to establish myself as an effective pan-Asian freelance journo, and on my return I began to write for the

Times. The old tensions between us had gone.

And so the departure from Streatham took place. My parents went to live in Mortlake: nice shops, the river, friends in the media close by, a much more comfortable shade of bourgeois. Duff was, alas, no longer with us, but Floss was now in situ, and my father took her for walks along the river. Once, while doing so, he took a small path that led off the towpath. Like Alice, he entered a magic world, an open-air treasure house.

This was Lonsdale Road reservoir, sometime known as the Leg o' Mutton reservoir – a small stretch of still water that lies just where the Hammersmith Bend unwinds if you are rowing in the Boat Race. It is overhung with trees, but has sudden vistas of open water. And on that water come birds. One of the great things about open water is that there is nothing to stop you seeing the birds; if they are there, you can see them. They don't keep getting hidden by leaves; they generally don't fly off the second you are in binocular range. On the water, they feel safe: they know you can't get them. The snag is that they are often quite a long way away, as I had discovered when staring at Staines reservoir with Shirtless Tim, looking at a distant black blob that would certainly be a scoter if it was quarter of a mile closer. But this stretch of water is tiny, 50 yards across at the most, and the birds came there in disproportionate numbers: cormorants, herons, swans, geese and lots and lots of ducks.

There is a lesson to be learnt here and we shall explore it later on. But enough to say that my father was filled with delight. This was birdwatching as it ought to be: you go for a walk, with the dog, and there the birds are. He had a pair of binoculars, which he had bought when visiting me in Hongkong, for no better reason than he thought it might be nice to have them. They were not much better than my horse-racing glasses, but they did indeed bring the birds closer.

And so, when I paid a family visit, I would bring my binoculars, and my father and I would walk round the reservoir together, and he would show me a crowd of shovelers with such pride you might have thought he had brought them all in himself. Thanks to Shirtless Tim, I was slightly ahead of him, and so I began to take the lead.

"Isn't that a female mallard?"

"I don't think so," I would say.

"For my money, it's a female gadwall. Observe the white speculum."

Nice word: I was impressed, anyway. A speculum is the distinctive patch of colour on the wing; the mallard has a blue one, and the gadwall white, male and female both. My father had never observed a speculum before; now he always does. It is a small part of that process of establishing an understanding of the birds. Not just birds: it was a rare thing we were doing. He had given me birds, now I was giving birds back to him. He was also, rather splendidly, able to overlook my occasional bouts of bossiness about speculums and so forth.

There were rafts in the middle of the reservoir. A lot of birds like them: surrounded by water, you are safe. And better than that, if you make your nest on a place surrounded by water, none of those hateful, land-bound creatures is going to eat your eggs or your chicks. You've got away from the bloody rats, in short. A raft is a Safe Place, and all animals, humans included, have a special feeling for Safe Places: a nice house in Mortlake, a nice raft in the middle of the water.

The rafts were put there by conservationists for that very reason; and plenty of birds made use of them for roosting and for nesting. But I knew that there was one bird in particular they wanted. And a season or so later, they came.

You may have seen tern without noticing them. Plenty of people have: seagull, they say, as a white bird flies past, a white bird with a black cap. But the habit of looking, the habit of watching, turns those seagulls into birds of spectacular beauty and perfection. I remember seeing them for the first time with my father, years before, when walking along the cliffs in Cornwall. We had acquired the habit of half-hearted, naked-eye birdwatching as we walked. I remarked that here was a pair of black-headed gulls. Instantly, they stopped dead in the air, hung there for a second and then arrow-dived into the sea. They were about as much like seagulls as Concorde is like a jumbo jet.

And there they were, over this funny little stretch of water on the rim of the Thames – sleek, elegant, fast, and prone to those reckless headlong dives, masters of the air. If black-headed gulls are the Neville brothers, a tern is David Beckham. So my father had a world of wonder on his doorstep, and I was able to drop by and share it. We had telephone conversations about the arrival of the terns, or the nesting of the pair of swans: local-patch birdwatching.

My mother wanted to buy my father a really special present. She had been ill for some time; perhaps she knew it would be her last present, and she wanted to make it a good one. She asked me to get him a pair of binoculars, and gave me a budget of £250. So I went to a specialist shop (another treasure house) and spent a happy half-hour peering across the road at pigeons and chimney pots and discussing the endless fascinations of optical glass, and I made a hideous mistake. I bought a pair of optically brilliant binoculars. But as with everything else, there is a payback. They weighed about as much as a dead albatross, and were about as pleasant to have around your neck. You can get the same quality in lighter binoculars: but for about two or three times the price. I was pleased with the brightness and vividness of the image, but as soon as I got them home, I knew they were wrong. So I went back and changed them – In Focus are a good firm to do business with – and I went for the exact opposite extreme. I bought a pair of Leica miniatures. They weigh little more than a dead wren and yet the image is stunning, sharp and clear. They are not as big and spectacular as the big jobs – but on the other hand, you'd always take them with you when you left the house.

It was a brilliant decision. To this day, my father scarcely leaves home without them: takes them to the opera, the reservoir, his favourite Cornish walks, and when he comes to visit me in Suffolk. They are perhaps the ultimate binoculars for a bad birdwatcher.

The combination was perfect; the reservoir and the binoculars combined to bring birdwatching into his life – not an occasional treat but as a matter of day-to-day living. And that, I think, is the principal aim of this book: to encourage every one who picks it up to look about, all the time, every day. Not obsessively scanning, just always aware. Everything else comes from looking. Birdwatching isn't something you do; it is something you are.

A rum coincidence, then, that, within the space of a few years, my father and I *both* became bad birdwatchers in this committed sense of being aware of birds as an enthralling aspect of daily life. Birds became a perpetual topic of conversation – I saw this today, that arrived yesterday, the first I'd seen this year, and I saw something that looked like this, what the bloody hell do you think it was?

Birds are life-enhancing: they bring joy when you see them, and it is a constant joy to share your life with them; and to share that joy with fellow-humans.

It would be easy and cheap and inaccurate to say that it was birds that brought me and my father together. No; time did that. Alcohol certainly helped – pints here and shared bottles.

Bad birdwatching was a shared aim at one stage; more than 20 years later it became a shared achievement, a shared joy. He was the teacher when we began; I was the teacher when we continued – make the old bugger interested in natural history. There are many better teachers, but I was at least there, and always a step or so ahead, thanks to Shirtless Tim and others we will meet in a chapter or so. But bad birdwatchers we were; and part of the joy was and is that it was a shared thing. It was a shared discovery and re-discovery, for we both got better at the same time; I don't recall any mad oedipal need to make sure I stayed ahead, but sharing my newly acquired knowledge was and still is one of life's quiet pleasures.

It would have been good enough had it been an interest in trains, but an interest in birds is something different. And I remembered that tern, that pair we saw years ago, plunge-diving into the Atlantic. Back in those days, my father and I would sometimes go for a spot of wild talk, generally over a third pint, or an additional bottle of wine; times when differences and disappointments had been submerged by the companionable glugaglug. We had a thirst, it seems to find something in common. And often, we would talk about walking the Cornish coastal path, the longest footpath in Britain, and we would say, well, why the hell not?

I remember we once mentioned this plan to an old family friend, a writer named Martin Worth. "We're talking about walking the Cornish coast path," my father told him over a vinous lunch. "And that's where it will end," Martin said expansively. "Talking about it."

Dipper

14. The right place

What a stroke of luck –
Hawk spied above
Irago promontory.

Basho

That reservoir was the clue. Place. It was the discovery of
the right place that propelled my father into the life of a
bad birdwatcher. Chance opened the door, and he walked
through spellbound. All bad birdwatchers who wish to
discover birds must discover place. In order to understand
birds – in order to see birds – you have to come to terms
with the idea of place. In order to meet all those birds

in the field guide – the ones that seem to be as rare as unicorns and hippogriffs and cockatrices – you have to know where to go.

Let's say you have never seen a dipper. Well, it's not your fault. It's not because you are too bad a birdwatcher to see dippers. You have read that they like streams, but they are never to be seen on the streams that you walk along. They are never around at that brook in the park; they are never there when you walk the dog along the Thames.

The fact is that dippers are extremely picky about the places they live. What I am about to say sounds obvious, I know, but it is the step that takes you to the next level of enjoyment of your birds. The fact is that you won't get to see different sorts of birds unless you go to different sorts of places. But birds are creatures of place. Some birds have a broad range of places they like – peregrine falcons like cliffs, but they can also put up with the ledges of city buildings, so long as there are plenty of pigeons for them to eat. Other birds are very specific. Like the dipper.

Mostly, they like fast-flowing streams with plenty of rocks, because they are odd little birds, like big fat wrens, except they have the unnerving habit of flying straight into waterfalls. And, if you go to the right sort of stream, you are almost certain to see a dipper, and if you walk along it for a way, you will see several. You will probably see the same one again and again as he flies away along the line of stream to avoid you – until he runs into the territory of the dipper next door and finds some way of doubling back. Find your stream, and you have found your dipper.

That is why the field guides tell you that they are common; and they certainly are, but only if you go to exactly the right sort of place. I remember visiting Fountains Abbey in Yorkshire, a wonderful and holy place. And I had an odd feeling that to complete the sense of perfection, the sense of sacredness of the place, what I wanted was a really nice bird. Not a frivolous wish. Blake, who clearly had never been much troubled by mosquitoes in the night, said: "Everything that lives is holy." And, strolling around the noble and pious ruins, I observed a shallow, swift-flowing, rocky stream and at once, I thought: "Hullo!" There had to be one. And sure enough, within a couple of minutes, I had my bird: dumpy, brown, dapper, busy. A dipper: right place, right bird.

I used to wonder why I never saw a nightjar. Field guides tend not to over-commit themselves, for the very good reason that birds often turn up in unlikely places. Any open country, you can read, is good enough for the nightjar. True: but you are highly unlikely to see them unless you go to the right sort of open country, the sort of open country that nightjars like very much indeed. Suffolk heathland is one of those places; and there I heard and saw them – two, no three together, just like the 49 bus.

Certain species, then, are pretty specific about what they need. Bearded tits are supposed to be pretty common, but you won't see them unless you visit a reedbed. And there are certain places that many different kinds of birds like an awful lot, while there are others that they don't like at all.

Capricious? Not at all. They need to find food, safety, and in breeding times, somewhere to meet and mate, lay an egg or two and rear some young. If a place doesn't supply those needs, then there won't be any birds there. You won't see many birds in intensive arable farmland, for the same reason that you won't see many humans in the middle of the Antarctic. There's no reason to go there: nothing to eat, nowhere to be comfortable. Intensive farmland is often and aptly called green desert, and it is no more capable of supporting a nice population of good fat birds than the Sahara. A great deal of the countryside is not nearly as good for birds as your local park, or, for that matter, your back garden.

But go to the right places, and a kind of explosion takes place before your eyes. It is as if all the world turns to birds. I remember the astonishing moment when I first opened the viewing flap of a hide at the RSPB reserve at Minsmere:

birds and birds and birds. Many avocets, that's what Minsmere is famous for, but many others as well. I have seen the common and the uncommon and the ludicrous at Minsmere. On a recent visit, a pair of spoonbill dropped in. Once I saw a flamingo. It was a Chilean flamingo, and it probably hadn't flown in all the way from Chile; there is a collection of Chilean flamingos not too far away and it was more or less certainly an escape. But it came to Minsmere; that's where the grub is. Some place are honey-pots, and birds positively swarm there.

All right, Minsmere is a bird reserve, and it is managed specifically so that birds will like it. But it was taken over by the RSPB because the avocets went there of their own accord; it was already a great place and conservation work has just made it better. And there are plenty of other places that birds come to, not because they are managed, but because they just happen to be good places to make a living in.

That is how nature works. An avocet is designed specifically to make a living in brackish lagoons – sieving and slashing through water for small beasts is exactly what its crazy upturned beak was designed for. Make a nice lagoon and if there are avocets within easy commuting distance, they'll come. The more such places, the more avocets there will be in the world, because they will breed more and their population will expand to fill the resources available.

Honeypots come in a diversity almost as astonishing as that of the birds that fill them. I've already mentioned Staines reservoir. Rubbish-tips and landfill sites are also honeypots: you see gulls in fantastic numbers; one thing that always stirs the heart is lots and lots of birds. The sight fills you with the feeling that humans haven't, after all, buggered up the entire planet quite yet. And if you can feel that sort of emotion at a rubbish-tip, what might you feel at a seabird nesting colony? Or a winter gathering of lapwing? Or a high-tide at an estuary when it is standing-room-only to huddling thousands of waders?

At such sights, it is hard to worry about identification and specific numbers. These are legitimate scientific concerns for a good birdwatcher. But what thrills bird-watchers good and bad is birds and birds and birds, and what great numbers say about the magic of place. The sacredness of place, if you prefer.

These days you don't just get field guides to the birds; you can get field guides to the fields as well. There are all sorts of where-to-watch-birds books. Some of these deal with the great sites across the country, or in other countries; others with the sites in a single county. There are some that are just about the birdy places, others tell you about general wildlife sites – places where you can look for nightingale, red deer, clouded yellow butterflies and southern marsh orchids. Get one, get several, make the visits; these books are yet another form of Alice's key, and will take you through magic doors into sacred places to meet extraordinary beings, often in incomprehensible numbers. Don't worry about why you never see a barn owl in your city park; make a pleasant journey to a pleasant place to where you have read that barn owls can be seen.

Look hard for them, but don't be too single-minded. Remember the law of the Ganges dolphin. And if you go to a place that's right for one fine beast, the chances are that it will be pretty good for others as well. Or, for that matter, instead. You're there to revel in nature, not to hunt for scalps, after all.

Place is mere common sense. If you want to see vast flocks of humans, it is better to go to New York than to East Coker or Little Gidding. If you want to see Romans, the best place to go is probably Rome. People have more chance of making a living and finding shelter in a big city; a better chance of breeding, too. So, if you want to see humans in good numbers, New York isn't a bad place to start. If you want to see plenty of birds, then Minsmere is a better bet.

The great thing about Minsmere is that it has an awful lot of different places in the one place. Different habitats, to be more technical: saline lagoon, reedbed, sea coast, river, water meadows, heathland, deciduous woodland. You won't get a spoonbill in the oak-trees or a blue tit in the reedbeds; but with a mixture of different places like this, you will get a very high number of species. And people have counted more than 100 in a day; me, best I've done is 80-odd in a morning.

As you get to watch birds more, you will get to learn about the places they like. Alas, you can't rely on birds entirely for their good taste: rubbish tips, as we have seen, are a favourite. So are sewage farms and nuclear power stations. It's true: the water used for cooling is released out at sea; this comes out a fair bit warmer than the surrounding sea, and so naturally the fish like it. Equally naturally, the fish-eaters like it. Nuclear power stations are great places for seeing seabirds.

Some bird places take a bit of getting used to. It's hard to get people excited about mud, but the mud of river estuaries is packed with food, and therefore packed with birds - thrilling numbers of long-legged bodies frantically busy trying to feed between tides, or crowded together at high water waiting for the cafeteria to reopen.

But in the main, all bird places are fabulous. The birds make them so. And just as there are thrilling moments in birdwatching, and there are times of quietly rewarding ordinariness, so there are ordinary places and there are extra-special places. Many of these extra-special places are called Sites of Special Scientific Interest. They are referred to by the hissing term of SSSIs. They are actually cathedrals: the most important and treasured part of our heritage. I have visited some that have been damaged beyond repair, I have visited others that are glorious and in their prime. SSSIs are not just for birds; some receive this designation because of their important plant communities, mammals, reptiles, butterflies. SSSIs are there - supposedly – to safeguard our natural wonders that are the heritage of us all.

These, then, are the cathedrals, but there are thousands more places of ordinary everyday loveliness. There are little corners of scruffiness in a disciplined desert of farmland, for example. Everywhere, there are small places that teem with birds of the ordinary and everyday kind. Start, if you like, with the little spinney behind my house. Or the pond on the common, or the scrubby bit of hawthorn on the railway line. Call these places the parish churches, hermitages, wayside shrines, chapels, oratories. Each one is jolly nice on its own, but it is the totality of these places that counts. They are ordinary and they are many, and, without them, there would be no birds and no life worth living for humans either.

These places are not valuable because birdwatching is a nice hobby. They are important because birds indicate life in its richness and its diversity, and without places where birds are, we would have a deeply impoverished planet. Without such places we are cut off from what makes us part of nature, and therefore we are cut off from what makes us truly alive.

Yes, places matter, and we should visit them as pilgrims and savour the richness they bring to our lives. And also we must revel in the places that are ordinary and local and agreeable, and revel in their ordinary everyday birds: the stroll in the park, the dog-walk, the evening ramble in the lighter months of the year. And, with them, we must revel in the exceptional and the extraordinary. Pay a visit, pay a homage to one of the great cathedrals, and you will feel the benefit of that visit for years to come. It's a few years ago, now, but I still have that 1,000-strong flock of lapwing I saw on a trip down to Sussex – the air filled with the sound of their oboe-calls; the smart green sheen of their backs so nicely set off against the white; the little curly crests, and that acrobatic, flop-winged flight.

The birds need these special places. They need them almost as much as we do.

Magpies ×

15. Bad birds

By the pricking of my thumbs,
Something wicked this way comes.

Macbeth

But perhaps you have reservations about magpies. An awful lot of people do. Or sparrowhawks, for that matter, but magpies get more hate-mail than any other bird. The RSPB gets more enquiries about magpies than anything else, which is odd considering that we live in a world working up to an ecological holocaust. Magpies, it seems, are taking over the countryside, killing everything in their way. They are incontrovertible proof that the world has gone horribly and irretrievably wrong.

"Oh, there used to be lots of birds here," people say. "Now we only have magpies." The magpies are to blame for killing all the nice songbirds. And they don't even eat the grown-up birds: being sneaky and cowardly and altogether loathsome, they eat the eggs and the babies. They are evil city-slicker child molesters, clad like a cad in correspondent shoes, cackling loudly and always with an air of being up to no good, like Private Walker in *Dad's Army*.

Many bad birdwatchers are filled with this anti-magpie prejudice, and they think that something should be done. They think magpies are a bad thing: they are bad birds, and need to be punished.

There are two separate errors here. The first is that some birds can be good and some can be evil. Birds are not humans. They no doubt have strict moral codes of a kind between themselves. Certain standards of behaviour are expected between members of a species – without them, the species wouldn't be able to get on, understand each other, mate, raise young. But you simply cannot impose human morals onto non-humans.

You can teach a dog not to lie on the sofa, but he won't see that as a moral prohibition. Being a dog and smart, he will work out pretty quickly that it is a bad idea to get caught, that sofas lead to telling-offs. And he will learn either to avoid sofas, or to get off them whenever he hears a footfall. It is a practical, rather than a moral, problem for a dog.

Magpies scavenge. Of course they do. They are very clever opportunists. They are not squeamish in any human understanding of the term. I have seen them peck open rubbish bags in a hunt for food; our stomach-turning leavings are Michelin three-star for a magpie. They feed on roadside corpses, taking the eyes first as a special treat. They will beak through dog-droppings for undigested edible bits.

All right, yuck. But they are not trying to be humans; they are succeeding very well at being magpies. And yes, they will take eggs and chicks. It is not their exclusive diet; they are omnivores. They take what they can get when they can get it. And yes, I drop this stance of lofty scientific detachment when I see a magpie going for a mistle-thrush nest and when the mistle thrushes, filling the air with a sound like a football rattle waved at the scoring of the greatest goal in history, turn on the magpie in parental fury. "Go on!" I find myself shouting. "Give it to the bastard!"

But then I am human, after all. The thing we humans find hard to believe is that nature is not there to please us. We are not, after all, lords of nature; we are just a part of nature. One more species, if a rather rum one. Nature is not organised for our special delectation. Much of nature is glorious – that is to say, profoundly pleasing to humans. But plenty of it is – or would be, if we were talking about human morality – pretty horrible.

But nature is not horrible. Nature is not wonderful. Nature is not cruel. Nature is not beautiful. Nature only is. And it is not our job to change it.

I saw a sparrowhawk the other day. It came into the garden flying fast and hard at zero feet, turned hard left into the bird-feeder, put the lot to flight, missed everything, and vanished. Wonderful bird; a wonderful moment.

It makes its living by eating other birds. It likes nut-feeders very much, because these are honeypots for the little birds it likes to eat. You put out your peanuts to help blue tits, and they help sparrowhawks to kill blue tits. Should that weigh heavy on your conscience? Should you stop doing it? Won't it help the blue tits to get wiped out?

No, no and no. The blue tits are perfectly capable of making their own decision about the pluses of food-gathering and the minuses of mortal danger. Life is always dangerous for blue tits. They must get food somehow, and it is a fact that bad winters and starvation kill far more blue tits than any sparrowhawk. Or, for that matter, magpie. Or, for that matter, domestic cats: and they, well-fed and pampered, are only killing for the sport.

Certainly, a sparrowhawk killing can be a distressing sight: a dying bird is a pitiful thing. If you don't find it heart-rending, you don't have a heart. I have had many a sad letter from gentle-souled people who have witnessed such sights at their beloved bird-table, and are deeply distressed by the existence of sparrowhawks and the amorality of nature. It's a hard life; most wild lives are pretty hard. But all the same, I'd sooner be a blue tit in a sparrowhawk-filled (and magpie-filled) wood than a chicken in a battery farm. Now that's what I call cruelty, but I won't turn your stomach here with tales of cannibalism and the de-beaking machine. Wild birds live a difficult and dangerous life, and that is precisely what they are good at.

Sparrowhawks are there to be admired, accepted, revelled in for their speed, agility and cunning. Nothing in nature is as good at moving fast through dense thickets, dodging, weaving, tucking in a wing here and turning on a dime there.

And sparrowhawks are rarer than blue tits, have you noticed? In fact, that is the most significant thing about them. In the same way, blue tits are rarer than caterpillars. In any bit of woodland, there will be far, far more caterpillars than blue tits. Blue tits eat caterpillars – blue tits, if you like, are cruel to caterpillars. They eat an awful lot of caterpillars, and yet there are still more that somehow survive. That is why there are butterflies as well as blue tits.

So in this wood, with its many-many caterpillars, there are many blue tits. But there is only one pair of sparrowhawks, and that's if you're lucky. That's if the wood is big enough. That's if the wood is big enough to hold enough caterpillars to hold enough blue tits to support the high and rarefied life of the top predator. The caterpillar can manage on just a branch. The blue tit can cope with just a few trees. But a pair of sparrowhawks needs a whole wood if they are to survive and raise little sparrowhawks.

Suppose you have a decent-sized wood, with its many-many caterpillars and its many blue tits and its one pair of sparrowhawks. And someone chops down half the wood to build some houses. Well, there will be still be many-many caterpillars and there will still be many blue tits. But there will be no sparrowhawks. The wood is now too small and there is not a big enough population of blue tits to keep them going.

Suppose you want to wipe out the caterpillars. Say it has been decided they are a health risk. And this is a big job, because there are so many; but you are at least half successful. So well done, you have killed half the caterpillars. As a result, you will find, to your sadness, that you have inadvertently killed half the blue tits. But you haven't finished here. You have killed off all the sparrowhawks as well. Every one. Quite by accident. It's the top predators who are the most vulnerable. The lives of those who eat are more precarious than the lives of those who are eaten.

It seems obvious that the predators control the population of prey animals; that the sparrowhawk controls the numbers of blue tits, the lion controls the number of wildebeest. But the exact opposite is true. I know it is counterintuitive, but it is the way things are. The number of lions is controlled by the number of wildebeest; the number of sparrowhawks is controlled by the numbers of blue tits. The vulnerable species in the wood is not the caterpillar, and not the blue tit, but the sparrowhawk. The bigger and fiercer you are, the rarer you are. The more vulnerable you are.

Which brings us back to magpies. For the same rule applies to them. I don't know where this myth about "all the songbirds are gone" has come from. When I lived in Barnet, there was a nice little patch of scrub behind our house. In and around it, there were plenty of magpies. There were also, in May, six different species of warbler. This was because it was a nice stretch of scrub with plenty of food and cover for the songbirds. Magpies or no magpies, they flourished, and the magpies flourished with them. The people who said there were no songbirds just didn't listen. They weren't even bad birdwatchers; they were just parroting a suburban myth. The place was absolutely heaving with songbirds, and it heaved with magpies as well.

There are places where songbirds really are in decline: but suburbia isn't one of them. It is out in the farmland that the problem lies, and it all comes down to changes in farming practice. There's not so much food lying around, so there are fewer skylarks and fewer song thrushes. And, partly as a result, fewer magpies.

If you go to a place where there are lots of magpies, it is highly likely that there will be lots of songbirds. If there were no songbirds, there would be no magpies. An animal doesn't survive for generation after generation by eating up the entire food supply (as the human species is coming to realise). If magpies had really killed all the songbirds, they would also have killed all the magpies. They would have made life impossible for themselves. But there are still magpies, and there are still songbirds.

Life is no more cruel than it is benign. Igor Stravinsky once said: "Music is, by its very nature, powerless to express anything at all. Music expresses itself." In the same way, life is not there to teach us moral tales, or to uplift us with its beauty or to appal us with its cruelties. Life is.

But, if the non-human world is not always beautiful, and is frequently difficult and distressing, then why do we turn to it? Why are we so keen on its beauties, so enthralled by its diversity? We humans are part of nature, and part of us responds very strongly indeed to the natural world. We are a species that is constantly reaching out to the world beyond ourselves.

Humans have a very strong affinity to other forms of life. This is not New Age stuff; let me say this once again. It is a matter of hard scientific fact. The phenomenon has been called "biophilia" by Edward Wilson, the scientist I mentioned before when I was going on about biodiversity.

Let's go back to New York. If you want an example of the cities' city, it's New York; more especially, Manhattan, with its glorious canyoned streets and avenues. And what is the most desirable, the most sought-after, the most expensive address in New York? Answer: Central Park. People flock to that cities' city, and, if they are rich enough, they live by the only bit of green they've got.

In carefully prepared psychological tests, people, when offered a choice of views of woodland, jungle, urban environments, cityscapes and so forth, have demonstrated a distinct – statistically inevitable – preference for park-like habitat: for wooded savannah, in fact, most especially if there is a nice bit of water. This is precisely the landscape in which humankind first walked upright.

Humans like to be on a prominence, with a nice view, where they can see the country and feel safe from danger, looking down on the nicely spaced trees and the patch of water below. Landscape architects appreciate this and the more they can construct a landscape that resembles this ideal, the more the property-men can sell for. People recover better from surgery if they have a window; better still if the window has a nice view of trees and open water.

In the United States, more people visit zoos than attend sporting events. In our language and our thoughts, we make the sharpest possible distinction between living and non-living; between cherts and blue tits. Children learn to speak with animal stories and animal sounds. The greatest leisure activity in this country is walking in the country; the most popular sporting activities are fishing and horse-riding. Britain is a nation of gardeners. We love to reach out beyond our own species; any one who has patted a dog, stroked a cat, given or received a rose knows that. In fact, I wish hotels would wake up to this idea. When checking in somewhere in the middle of a long trip, I would like to be asked: "Smoking or non?"

"Non, please."

"Cat or non?"

"Cat please."

Just imagine. A long day out there doing my stuff, and back to the hotel: a book, the duty free and, best of all, a cat to scratch behind the ears. It would bring the day back into focus; I would be earthed. It may be possible to construct a world without other creatures to share it, but I'm damned if I'd want to live in it.

This last couple of hundred years is the first in which humans have seriously considered themselves capable of living apart from nature. The more this notion is pursued, the more hungrily we seek nature. Birdwatching is not a hobby, not a form of trainspotting. It is nothing less than a way of reclaiming our own. Wilson says: "Signals abound that the loss of life's diversity endangers not just the body but the spirit. If that much is true, the changes occurring now will visit harm on all the generations that follow."

A hefty conclusion to reach from the starting point of a packet of peanuts. But an inescapable one.

House Martins

16. The right time

And greenfoot slow
She moved among
The sea—ea—ea-sons.

Robin Williams/The Incredible String Band

My understanding of birds and their sense of place was enhanced by a year I spent at Minsmere: how could it not? It was one of the great cumulative birdwatching experiences. I was researching a book about a year in the life of the old place (published a decade and more back as *Flying in the Face of Nature*). I hope the book was all right. I can tell you without false modesty that the research was quite brilliant. It put me on terms of intimacy with exceptional birds, exceptional bird-people and a quite exceptional place. If SSSIs are the cathedrals of the natural world, then Minsmere is York Minster.

People have often asked what I like best about my year in Minsmere, and I always answer "Tuesday". The reserve is closed to the public on Tuesdays, to allow the staff and volunteers to get on with more in-your-face conservation activities than is appropriate when there are visitors about. But, very generously, I was allowed to come on Tuesdays, and I thrilled to the pleasures of having the place to myself. And the birds, of course.

The warden at the time was Jeremy Sorensen, a fellow not without his eccentricities. He is a man with a clever and perverse mind and a great gift for thinking bird: for seeing bird, understanding what birds need and working out how to give it to them. He had an odd relationship with visitors, too. Minsmere these days is a honeypot for people as well as birds; and you can enter a hide and find it full to bursting in the high season. Someone wrote a letter of complaint: there were people in the hide, he said, who didn't even have binoculars.

"Good!" said Jeremy. "That's who we want. We don't want you, we've already got you. People without binoculars are the people we are looking for." In other words, the future for birds lies with bad birdwatchers. That's something to bear in mind as we march towards our conclusion.

Jeremy used to get fed up with the po-faced seriousness of good birdwatchers, whispering speculative identifications to each other at the back of a hide. People always whisper in a hide, not because they don't want to disturb the birds or the birdwatchers, but because they don't want to be overheard misidentifying a bird.

"Look!" Jeremy would say in a sudden booming voice, making everybody jump, "A seagull!"

But perhaps Jeremy's favourite tease was to ask his August visitors: "How are you enjoying your autumn holidays?" They would respond in necessary bafflement, and Jeremy would explain that so far as the birds were concerned, spring was over and autumn had begun. In Jeremy's calendar, summer's lease hath no date at all. It was his thesis that there were only three seasons: spring, when birds meet, mate and breed; autumn, when they shift from these activities to those of movement and regrouping, essentially a period of transition, and winter. Endless winter in which the birds hang on in the hope of breeding again come the spring.

As a simplification it is very useful, and the combination of this Sorensenism, and the fact that I spent a full year visiting Minsmere on a more or less weekly basis, led to a discovery every bit as important as the discovery of place. It was nothing less than the discovery of time.

Birds do not spend their life hanging about hoping to be spotted by bad birdwatchers. They have urgent priorities of their own. And at the top of the list is breeding. The aim of every living thing is to become an ancestor; that is what evolution means. If you have bred beings that will survive and breed in their turn, you have made your mark. Your genes carry on. That is why there is joy unconfined for every human who becomes a grandparent. Everything a bird does is centred around the same urge. And so they sing, gather food, fly in great flocks, huddle together on bitter days. All these are methods of getting ready for breeding: steps towards the great goal of becoming an ancestor. If a bird – any living thing – leaves a single breeding descendant then, in evolutionary terms, that life has not been in vain. And it is that urge that dictates all these other matters of place and time.

When do you breed? First, when there is enough food to feed yourself, for you need to be on the very top of your form to win a mate, hold a territory, build a nest, lay eggs, feed chicks. And second, when there is enough food for your young. So naturally, you attempt to coincide your breeding with the time of the greatest abundance of food. The blue tits nest when there are most caterpillars, the sparrowhawk when there are most blue tits. For both of them, that has to be spring, and that makes spring the most thrilling time of the year – and it begins far earlier than you dare imagine. If it is a mite depressing to be told that August is the middle of autumn, it is positively exhilarating to detect unambiguous signs of spring in early January: a hard, clear, cold morning after a frosty night and there, singing his spring song with all his heart, a mistle thrush. The wild song, the courage and defiance of this bird, brings us one of the great moments of the year. January is the season of death – in the midst of it this, the mistle thrush carol of life and hope. I once heard woodlark sing on December 20; now that is a seriously early call for spring.

The ever-lighter days of the passing winter are filled with increasing signs of spring. "One by one the chorus swells, till it's a mighty sound," sing the Incredible String Band in a song about birdsong, and that is what happens in slow motion throughout the spring. It is a process that starts in January (December if you're a crazy woodlark) and reaches its climax in May.

When breeding is done – and some birds will go through two and even three broods – there comes the strange autumn time: the great diaspora. Birds don't sing in order to fill us with joy – our joy is just a rather agreeable by-product – but to attract mates and defend territory. When breeding is done, most have no further need for song or territory, and so they fall silent and the family disperses. Robins are rare exceptions: they will defend feeding territories throughout the winter, and sing to warn off allcomers. That's why, even in the darkest days, you hear the sweet lisping song of a robin. Remember that: listen in winter, and if you hear a bird singing, it's almost certainly a robin. That's the second bird-song you will learn, after cuckoo.

But most birds disperse. Some species form big winter flocks, there being safety in numbers; often, too, there are large food resources that large numbers can exploit. Privacy is put away for another year. The idea of winter is to hold on for another go at breeding, so you need to go where the food is. Birds move across the county to various favoured places.

And of course, some birds leave altogether and fly elsewhere, to somewhere warmer, but not for the sake of the warmth. They go for the food. Meanwhile, birds from further north come south to stay with us for the winter: the estuaries are full of waders who have flown down from Scandinavia and elsewhere, to use the rich resources that lie under the mud at the river-mouths. You can see them in mind-numbing numbers, like passengers waiting for a tube train, till a bird of prey makes a pass over them and puts them all into the air – so many, you can't believe that they don't keep bumping into each other and knocking each other out of the sky.

Autumn brings all kinds of oddities: when migration goes wrong it can go disastrously so. Most perish in the sea and the wind, but the odd straggler makes it here from North America, from Siberia, from elsewhere, and these windblown vagrants bring joy to the twitchers. Autumn is their favourite season: a restless time of movement and regrouping; preparation for the long period of hanging-on.

And then the hanging-on ends and overlaps with the beginning of the new spring. And as the spring progresses, the birds that left us in the autumn come back to fill our hearts with delight. For me, the first house martin that comes back to my house is like an airport meeting – that unbelieving first sight, that moment you knew was coming but hardly dared to believe in. Instead of the embrace by the abandoned luggage trolley, I tend to bellow and call for the family: Come out! Look! See who's come home!

And the martins will build their nests under the eaves, and, if it's a dry spring, I will water the ground in front of the house so they can find enough mud to make their own little cup-shaped houses, and I will watch them spinning round the house in a dizzy carousel as they sort out who is going to live where. And then they mate and breed and fly around the house making their little farting calls to each other. And they will breed again, in a good year, and in an exceptional year once more: so that sometimes, when autumn is here, I have seen as many as 80 line up on the telegraph wire. Funny. There weren't that many in April. And they chatter to each other, no doubt asking the way to Africa, and you notice that there are not quite as many as there were last week, and then one day you say: bloody hell, I haven't seen a martin for more than a week. Spring is gone, autumn is here.

I have been to Africa many times, and have seen the air full of swallows: European swallows, our swallows, swallows that might have nested in your garage. And African birdwatchers have the cheek to say that swallows are African birds that happen to breed in Europe. We say that they are European birds that happen to spend their winters in Africa.

This migration thing is something to get your head round. I have a special love of swifts. They are among the last arrivals: they don't come until spring is an accomplished fact. You know the season is at its height when the swifts are here, flying in on sickle-wings. They will breed here and the young will learn to fly, and eventually they leave their nests. They take to the air as fish to water. They feed on the wing, sleep on the wing, live and have their being on the wing. They are the most commitedly aerial of all birds. They even copulate on the wing: body to body, tumbling over and over, through thousands of feet; a must for anybody's reincarnation wish-list.

In July, the young birds take to the air like hooligans, and fly about screaming hysterically at each other; in mad circles, in wild forays down the main streets of towns, in spirals so high you can scarcely tell if they are birds, let alone swifts, but all the same, you know them for what they are. Only swifts love the sky that much, and seem to be loved back by the sky in return.

And after filling the air with the wild delight of being alive, they are gone, as suddenly and as dramatically as they had arrived. They live off the small creatures that fill the air: insects, parachuting spiders on lengths of silk, all the tiny beasts called aerial plankton. And you can't find that sort of stuff in this country in the winter, so off they go: south, for warmth, company, food.

And as they reach their homes in southern Africa they bring joy of a different kind. They come surfing in on the weather fronts, high, high above, with a screaming you can hear but distantly, if at all: little familiar specks in an altogether unfamiliar sky of blue-black fury. It is as if they are towing the rains behind: and Africans rejoice at the sight. The rainbirds are here, the rains are not far behind; blessed relief from the heat and the fierce flash-bulb light is almost upon them. The end of what old hands call "the suicide months" is here and it will soon be the time of cool and comfort and growth. Wherever swifts arrive, they bring good news. The best.

Time matters. Go to Minsmere in spring to see the birds breeding, defending territories. See the fluffy chicks – is there anything quite as charming as a new avocet, with its tiny retroussé beak? The Scrape, the most famous part of the reserve – the place where you find the avocets – is teeming, teeming with food, teeming with birds eating it and using it as fuel to breed. Go back in autumn and the avocets are gone, and other odds and sods drop by, some for a long stay, others to refuel on their way elsewhere. And in winter, there are times when the Scrape is untenanted: once I saw nothing but a crow on this, the most famous bit of habitat in British birdwatching. But in the spring; the wet meadows known as the Minsmere Levels are pretty quiet; in winter, they are crowded with gulls and geese, thousands of them. If you go looking for birds, you need to understand about place and about time.

And as you begin to understand time, you begin to understand the rhythm of the year as the birds understand it – as the birds live it. Understanding time is not just the key to seeing more birds. If you understand the year as a bird does, you have taken a step outside the human narrowness of vision. As you understand a bird's vision of time, you find you have begun to understand how the earth itself lives and breathes.

Great Tit

17. I spy with my little ear

Be not afeard: the isle is full of noises,
Sounds and sweet airs, that give delight, and hurt not.

The Tempest

My father rang me the other day. "Teacher!" he said.
"Teacher, teacher, teacher!" And I was filled with a
complex delight: pleasure in his pleasure, pleasure in the
sharing, joy in the coming spring, and the special joy that
comes from a teacher-pupil relationship.

But he was not addressing me as teacher. He was
imitating the spring song of the great tit. When winter
sends a day of unexpected brightness, of unseasonable

warmth, then a great tit finds his juices stirring, and instead of giving his usual contact calls and alarm calls, he will burst into a song. It is not a great song, as these things go, but it is bright, strident and optimistic; and it comes wonderfully early in the year. It is winter's death-knell: and though winter takes a long time in dying, its fate is sealed from the moment the great tit sings.

The call is brassy, disyllabic and clear – a strong stress on the first syllable: <u>tea</u>cher, <u>tea</u>cher, <u>tea</u>cher! Great tits have a huge range of song and call; one of the important rules of birdwatching is that, if you ever hear a bird-sound you have never heard before, it's a great tit. But that teacher-teacher song is utterly characteristic and quite unmistakable.

They sing teacher-teacher because it is spring, but that is not the precise reason why they sing. They sing because spring is the time for breeding. And many birds hold the belief that the best way to breed is to claim a territory, woo a mate and defend both against allcomers. And many of these birds believe that the best way to do so is in song.

Sing out! It is a challenge, a plea, a bit of showing-off, a bit of passion, a bit of lust, a bit of joy, a bit of fear. And note this: each species sings in its own way. They do this for the same reason that (most) birds look quite different: to tell each other apart. A great tit is not trying to chase away a blue tit; they are not competing for the same things. Still less is it trying to woo a blue tit. A blue tit's song is distinctive – thin and rather hurried. A great tit's song is big and noisy beside it, and many great tits have a number of variations. There is evidence to suggest that the more variations you have, the sexier you are: that a male with a fine repertoire will get the female he wants, the territory he wants.

It follows then, that humans, whose lives are dominated by ears and eyes, rather than nose, will be able to listen and come to some kind of an understanding of all this. And it is true. You can tell one bird from another with your ears. So let me tell you about a young entomologist lying in a tent in the middle of Africa wondering what the hell was keeping him awake. He had to know. Nobody could help him, for all that he was part of a scientific party. And so, haunted as never before, he resolved to find out. It was some years before he was able to put a name to the sound that started his lifelong pilgrimage. And it wasn't a bird at all. It was a tree hyrax: a mammal, a thing a bit like a guineapig, except that it is confusingly related to elephants. And it makes the most ungodly screaming sound that rises in pitch and intensity and speed until it reaches a wild rhythmic climax. I know; I have heard recordings that the said entomologist made, and I have heard the hyraxes for myself on the rim of the Ngorongoro crater. It was wacky enough for me, knowing where this mad sound came from; as a nameless sound of the night, it filled a young entomologist's entire soul.

The entomologist was Bob Stjernstedt, and as a result of the seed planted in his ear by the insane din of the tree hyrax, he has devoted his life to the sounds of African birds. He had to do it the hard way: hear a call, and then identify the bird by visual means. He has made tape recordings of species all over the continent, using a parabolic reflector he made himself. He specialised in Zambia, where he lives. And it was from Bob that I learned how to listen. Bob is said by some to be eccentric, but I would face a charging lion with him. In fact, I have already done so, but that must be a story for another day, preferably around a campfire with a bottle or two of Mosi beer. Far more frightening, I once faced a charging train with him on a single track railway bridge over a river in Wales: not a good moment.

But Bob gave me ears. What would you sooner be, blind or deaf? Discussion point in sixth form common rooms across the land; but in a way, most of us are already both: nature-blind, nature-deaf. This book has an evangelical purpose as strident as a great tit's song, and it is to hand you, dear reader, the chance to throw off this blindness, this deafness. I have written a lot about being bird-aware, of bringing birds into your life by acquiring the habit of looking. A small understanding of what you see goes a long way – telling one bird from another adds to their meaning and their beauty.

It is the same with sound. In a sense, it is a whole new sense I am offering. Instead of hearing a pleasant din, I am offering you the chance to identify the instruments of the orchestra, come to terms with the themes and the leitmotifs they play, and to have a decent stab at understanding the mind of the composer.

It is also the most wonderful conjuring trick, deeply satisfying to acquire. You walk beneath the canopy of a patch of wood in the spring. The birds, busy and involved, are all out of sight. But they sing: robin, you say, blue tit, great tit, song thrush, blackbird. They are as distinct as the voices of your nearest and dearest, people who do not need to say their names on the telephone. "Hello, it's me," says the song thrush.

You thought that great spotted woodpeckers were unusual; but, once you learn their pik-pik contact call, you know they are all around us, more or less wherever there are deciduous trees – high, busy, invisible. And by knowing the birds from their sounds, it is as if you had plucked them from your sleeves; as if, walking through a loud but empty wood, you had waved a wand and filled it with creatures of beauty and wonder, colour and perfection. You feel something beyond the pleasure of the magician; almost the pleasure of the creator, as if these birds that sing are somehow part of yourself.

The chorus swells from January until its reaches its crescendo in mid-May. And in March, you will hear another disyllabic harbinger of spring: not teacher-teacher but chiffchaff, two syllables of equal weight: chiff... chaff... chiff... chaff... , a somewhat monotonous song, but a great one for all that, because it means that the first of the migrants is here; the first big traveller has landed and is ready to claim territory and breed. And soon the others are following thick and fast. One of the annual great moments is the first willow warbler, that gorgeous, sibilant descent down the scale. It has flown in from southern Africa: an awfully long way for an awfully small pair of wings.

And yes, you may remember that I was talking earlier about the way in which willow warblers and chiffchaffs are almost impossible to distinguish; and that experts can be fooled, even when the willow-chiff is a bird in the hand. But hear them sing: they might as well be an eagle and a humming-bird, they are so different. And suddenly, all those identical looking little browny-olivey birds can be told apart: the answer is not in your eyes but your ears.

Cetti's warbler: look it up – it seems far too hard a bird for a bad birdwatcher. But their song is wonderful, loud and utterly distinctive. Go to the right place at the right time, and the chances are you will find your Cetti. You will see him if you have a great deal of patience and/or luck, but you will almost certainly hear him.

I was at a bird reserve in Cornwall with my father, and we were hunting for Cettis. A trousered lady with barbered hair addressed me pleasantly, if sternly: "I can't remember what a Cetti's warbler sounds like," she said. "Can you help?"

"Yes," I said. "I have a mnemonic. But it contains an obscene word."

She looked at me with a very faint smile: "I'm a medievalist."

I gave her a faint smile back. "Me? Cetti? If-you-don't-like-it-fuck-off." She thanked me. I had given her a mnemonic that gives the sense of the thing, along with the meaning and the rhythm and the tone.

And all this I taught my father. I was his teacher-teacher. We walked around his Thames-side reservoir and I made it a new place for him: "Blackbird," I would say. And he would listen, and nod. Got that one. "Reed warbler."

"How do you know it's not a sedge warbler?"

"Because reeds stand up straight, and sedge is more

tangled. Reed warblers are much more rhythmic. Reed warblers sound more like reeds." A bit of a tangled way of remembering, but it works. Got that one, too.

How do you set about acquiring this knowledge? It is harder if you don't have a guru. I had Bob to open my ears, but he taught me African bird sounds, not necessarily a help, since the incidence of trumpeter hornbill in East Anglia is small. Jeremy Sorensen at Minsmere was an inspiration and did an awful lot to help; but I did most if it myself.

And it was easy enough. All it took was a bit of mild obsessiveness. I did it with tapes. I listened, replayed and replayed, and spent a lot of time at Minsmere and round about where I lived in Hertfordshire, and I listened. And, haltingly, I began to find my way.

There are all kinds of resources available to get you started – and the whole thing is about getting started. Once you know half-a-dozen calls you are up and running. Naturally, the rules of time and place work for sound just as they do for sight; you'll hear one sort of sound in a deciduous woodland in May, quite another on an estuary in January.

But get started. I have supplied some contact details at the back of the book, where you can make a decision on what tape or CD to buy. Some of these are for reference:

look up the species, hear the call. Others are "atmosphere recordings" which give you a soundscape of birdsong. You can also get things like tinkling waterfalls, crashing waves and songs of the whales, which are supposed to be frightfully calming. These can be pleasant enough: I occasionally listen to CDs of African bush sounds, which take me right back to my favourite places. But there are also instructional tapes and CDs, and this is what you want to start with: a beginner tape that will give you the commonest bird you will hear from your garden or the park.

And I listened to tapes, and I walked and listened to birds, and got the garden birds clear in my mind and went on from there, and now my ears are always opened. Last night, a real old din from little owls; and I remembered one night, some years ago, opening the windows the better to hear the most extraordinary concert, one that involved at least three tawny owls, at least two barn owls and half-a-dozen or more little owls: all, for some reason, excited out of their minds and filling the air with the most wonderful cacophony.

And today a song thrush, for spring is now upon us out there. The song thrush is in love with repetition: it finds a nice phrase, gives it to you two, three or four times, and then abandons it for something else. They love the familiar, they love the new, just like bad birdwatchers.

The beginning of an understanding of song and call opens more Alice's doors than anything else in bird-watching. I used to wait on Hadley Wood station and see how many birds I could identify before the train came, and had a personal best of 18. Almost all recognised on call. I have taken part in bird races, when you try and identify as many birds in a day as possible: and most of that you do with your ears.

More importantly, in terms of actual science, I have identified birds by sound in the Northwest Province of Zambia, and, in the course of a few days, discovered 55 species that had never been recorded before in two adjoining 30 x 30 kilometre squares. It was a small but useful contribution to the ornithological atlas of Zambia. In a country as under-birdwatched as Zambia, even a bad bird-watcher is better than none.

Of course, I was with Bob Stjernstedt. What about the time he drove off the pontoon into the Luangwa river because he saw a small brown wader on the opposite shore (that one's not true, he always says)? What about the time he drove his friend's new Land Cruiser into the Bangweulu swamp (that one really is true)? What about the time he climbed up a tree to see a nest, fell out and lay out in the bush all night, a place filled with wandering hyenas renowned for their ability to bite the face off a sleeping man, only to walk into a nearby camp the following day covered in blood and casually asking for a beer?

Well, Bob is a man around whom legends accumulate. I used him as the basis for a character in a novel, but I toned him down shamefully. I was striving to write something believable. Bob brushes his hair every month whether it needs it or not, his shirt and trouser-crotch are always a crochet pattern made by the tumbling coals of his roll-ups, and he frequently wears two pairs of glasses at once, at least one of which has been fixed by Sellotape.

I had a few days at the end of a cricket trip, and I went to visit him in Livingstone, by the Victoria Falls. I had in mind a couple of days of gentle birdwatching: scour the gorges for falcons, try and find a taita, and amble along the fringes of the Upper Zambezi looking for finfoot.

I have known Bob 15 years, and should have known better. He met me at the airport with his expedition Land-Rover all ready loaded up, eight jerrycans pad-locked to the roof-rack. Pausing only to fill them up with diesel and to stop at the supermarket for a bottle of J&B, we hammered off along one of the tributaries of the Zambezi, picking up a track more or less where the map gives up.

After an awful lot of miles we made a camp by the

Zambezi, and made a start on the whisky. Next day, miles further on, we stopped at a rather fine open plain and recorded what he could find. Including the silent cloud cisticola – a bird we picked up, believe it or not, by song. (Incidentally there is a bird called the invisible rail, which I have never seen, but I least I have heard the silent cloud cisticola.) Cisticolas are yet more little brown jobs: there are more than 70 of them, and they all look the same. But they sound quite different. Bob is an expert on cisticolas: "Now if this was a *cloud* cisticola," he said.

"As opposed to a silent cloud?"

"Precisely. The nearest known population of cloud cisticola is about 300 miles away. So that would be really rather exciting."

Bob played me a recording of both species, and we drove on. And on. MMBA, the old Africa hands say, Miles and Miles of Bloody Africa. Brian Jackman, a wildlife writer, puts it rather better: "You can't believe that the country would ever end, or that you would ever want it to."

And another plain. Stop the vehicle. Get out. Listen. Look.

And then, clear as dawn, a cloud cisticola. A mystery: high in the cloud, as good as his name, circling around the plain, proclaiming his name and his ownership and his love for his mate. Exciting? It was joy of a very high and rarefied kind. It took a mere three hours or so of trampling about the plain from one side to the other until we got a proper a look at the damn bird, recorded all the plumage details, colour of its toenails etc, for this was another spot of science intruding into my life as a bad birdwatcher. God, scientists tell us, dwells in the details; and we record-ed minute details of time and place and plumage and voice: one bird, his mate, and their nearest friends that anybody knows about 300 miles away.

Bob and I had pushed back the frontiers of ignorance: pushed them back by the length of a micron or so. Human-kind knows a tiny, tiny bit more about the planet it lives on than it did before, and it was all thanks to me. Or rather to Bob, but I was there to play Tonto. I deserve some of the credit. I had paid for the diesel and the whisky, had I not? That was, in a weird way, deeply pleasing. That night I cooked up a hearty beany broth with plenty of chillies, and we drank a fair amount more of the J & B. Sounds of the night all round us. Exciting indeed.

A reasonably extreme way to appreciate bird sound, it is true. But let's have another example. Another whisky, too. Why not? My father and I were drinking it, and it was Glenmorangie, never a mistake. And we were talking about birds and about birds he had seen in Cornwall – peregrine falcons, back in numbers we had never known before:

thrilling birds, a thrilling thing to know.

And he remarked: "You know, if we don't do that Cornish walk soon, it's going to be hard to manage it with a Zimmer. And harder still for you to push me in a wheelchair."

"It has to be in May," I said.

And it was. May, best for birdsong. We walked from Newquay to Rinsey over the course of a week, stopping in pubs and B&Bs, lunching off a pasty and a pint, dining off pub food and more pints. Ales are very important on such a trip. We walked the majestic cliffs, fulmars to our right – that is to say, the seaward side – fulmars are related to albatrosses and fly with something of an albatross's nonchalance; and skylarks on our left. And peregrine and raven and tern and egret and, yes, that was the trip when we met the medievalist and the Cettis, and it was a week filled with birds and birdsong, pasties and ale. And talk.

We had a side bet, just for mustard. A bottle of Glenmorangie to the person who spotted the first seal. This led to a lot of looking at rocks. Was that a head rising above the waters, or was it the heaving sea falling back round an unmoving rock? Always it was the latter. It was on the last day that I won. I stayed looking just a mite too long at one of those heaving rocks.

"No bloody seals there, boy," my father said, with the unshakable confidence that has shaped his life.

I looked in unspeakable delight at the rock's whiskers, its fine bright eye. "Pick up your bloody bins."

He did so. "You bastard!"

Well, he should know.

Marsh Harrier

18. Let them be left

All you need is love.

John Lennon and Paul McCartney

Don't you hate it when you're watching a nice wildlife documentary, and you have been enjoying a pleasant visit to Eden, when suddenly, just as you get to the last bit and you're feeling quite good, the music goes all menacing, and the commentator says: "But this wildlife paradise is under threat. Even here, wildlife must pay the price for human progress. Human greed, human carelessness and human indifference are making mincemeat of these lovely furry animals. For Christ's sake, the whole bloody planet's gone wrong, and it's all your bloody fault, you smug bastard sitting there on your nice bloody sofa with your nice bloody drink within six inches of your guilty, bloodstained bloody hand."

Well, I'm not going to end the book this way. I am going to make the assumption that you already know about as much about the ecological holocaust as you want to – though do bear in mind, please, that the reality is ten times worse than you thought.

But there is a worse crime than crass destruction, and it is crass despair. It is giving up. For there is an answer to despair, and it is out there hanging upside down on your bird-feeder. Where there is life there is hope, and vice versa.

Liking birds is not just a nice thing to do. To look at a bird and feel good about it is a violent revolutionary act. To put out peanuts is an act of insurrection. It is an act that demands a revolution in political thought, for it is quite obvious that conservation is far, far too low on the political agenda.

It took Margaret Thatcher herself to point this out. She said gloatingly at the time of the Falklands War: "It's exciting to have a real crisis on your hands, when you have spent half your political life dealing with humdrum things like the environment."

Yes, we're destroying the planet, how frightfully dreary, how terribly *vieux jeu*. Far more exciting to have a little spat with gunboats, one famously described by Jorge Luis Borges as "two bald men fighting over a comb". The environment ought to be right at the top of the political agenda, because 100 per cent of us live in it. It is, I think, important for the future of the human race to have an environment. This is not a matter to leave to our grand-children; we must take it on now, if our grandchildren are to have anywhere to live, and anywhere worth living in. If we want to become ancestors (the goal of life, as any blue tit will tell you) then we should leave a viable world for our descendants, for our genes. But that's democracy for you: what everybody really wants is not something that ever gets much of a look in. Politicians think that five years is a dizzy plunge into the future; and what profit do they get from planning for the 22nd century?

However, I will give you three reasons for looking after the planet:

1. Because it's our duty. Humans are unique animals, in that we have control over the future of the planet. We owe it to the other species to look after them and their planet we share.

2. Because it's in our own best interests. Soiling your nest is never a good long-term policy. If we carry on poisoning the planet, we will carry on poisoning ourselves and our descendants.

3. Because we really, really want to. We have an affinity for species other than our own (biophilia) and we would be miserable in a planet without such things.

There is a trinity of reasons for conservation, then: duty, self-interest, and love. The greatest of these is the last: "The love that moves the sun and other stars", last line of The *Divine Comedy*, and it is something that you can renew with every glance from the window. Thus you start by looking at blue tits and you end up with a religion, a moral crusade and a political commitment.

So what to do about it? What can you do to make the world a better place? Looking at birds is the first step, and a highly potent one it is, too. The next move is to join the Royal Society for the Protection of Birds. This organisation not only runs nice bird reserves (in itself a powerful political statement) but also lobbies the government. It has an important part in the environment debate: sober, responsible, insistent, impeccably researched, unstridently expressed, highly respected – and at heart utterly radical.

For it is nothing less than radical to believe that the environment is a matter of the foremost importance.

If you are already a member of the RSPB, then join a second organisation: your county wildlife trust, the Worldwide Fund for Nature. The choice is large and all organisations have their different virtues. If you seek active involvement, then that is easy enough to do. I have put some useful contacts at the back of the book.

I believe we should all make a double commitment: to belong to one more thing (duty), and to do one more thing on a regular basis – to enjoy birds (love). The self-interest we can take as read.

Oh Lord, I can hear the beginnings of doubt in your mind. But listen: public opinion does actually make a difference. It was public pressure that brought about the end of CFC-emitting aerosols; it was public pressure across Europe that ended the dumping of radioactive waste at sea; it was public pressure that outlawed commercial whaling across the world; it was public pressure that led to the worldwide restrictions on trade in wildlife; it was public pressure that stopped genetically modified crops from taking over the landscape.

Another thing the doom'n'gloomers never point out is that there are good news stories as well as bad. Here are ten species, seven mammals and three birds, that – against all the odds – are not going to go extinct this week.

1. Giant panda

Still endangered, still on the brink, but still hanging on, in the most crowded country on earth. Destruction of their forest habitat has been stopped. There is genuine will from the Chinese government for the panda to survive. Not dead yet.

2. Marsh harrier

Extinct as a breeding bird in this country, because marshes were drained. Like all birds of prey, they were routinely shot and DDT in the food chain affected the top predators most. Now DDT is illegal in this country, so is persecution, marsh harriers are thriving and I have seen one from my house.

3. Southern right whale

With the end of commercial whaling and the break-up of the Soviet Empire (biggest whalers), the whales are coming back. It has been estimated that the southern right whale is increasing at nine per cent a year.

4. Eurasian otter

Hunted, shot, living in rivers so poisoned that the fish were all dying; the otter was on the way out. Now with cleaner rivers and less persecution plus active conservation, they are coming back. Every year more British river-miles have otters.

5. Whooping crane

This is a migratory bird of extraordinary beauty, commuting between Canada and the United States, and in 1941, they were down to 15 or 16. Habitat destruction, especially of the places where they stop to refuel on migration, was the main reason. Now there are 140 wild birds and three flocks in captivity.

6. Mauritius kestrel

Island species are both unique and uniquely vulnerable: a small disaster can wipe out an entire species. Habitat destruction was again the problem, but in 1973 a conservation programme began. The population was down to six; now there are around 300 and growing.

7. Juan Fernandez fur seal

A population of millions was reduced to extinction, or so it was thought, killed for meat and for their skins. Nothing was done at all to save them, but a global distaste for wearing sealskin and for slaughtering seal pups was enough. They are now back to 12,000 or so.

8. Arabian Oryx

This lovely animal – as near to a unicorn as you will ever see – really did go extinct in the wild, mainly through hunting. But an international effort saw a captive herd raised in Phoenix Zoo, and a re-release programme backed by the Sultan of Oman. They're back and booming.

9.White rhinoceros

The white rhino was brought to the brink by hunting and by the Chinese medicine trade. Now there are about 7,000, the bulk of the population in South Africa, where they are heavily guarded.

10. Siberian tiger

This is the biggest sub-species of tiger. It was thought that they were down to 200, but a recount brought them up to 500. The reason they are difficult to count is the reason they survive in decent numbers: the place where they live is still seriously wild.

So no, conservation is emphatically not moving deck-chairs on the *Titanic*. It works, both with and without human help. Sometimes human neglect is good enough. Time for some more from Gerard Manley Hopkins:

What would the world be, once bereft
Of wet and wildness? Let them be left,
O let them be left, wildness and wet;
Long live the weeds and the wilderness yet!

So I am planning a trip to my favourite place of weeds and wilderness, of wildness and wet, which is the Luangwa Valley in Zambia. I have been going there on and off for 15 years, and I have seen wonders beyond counting. But this trip will be different. I will be going with Joe. He'll be ten when we go. It seems that I have made the boy interested in natural history; though it is mammals rather than birds that make the earth move for him. "What are our chances of seeing a genet?"

"Ninety-five percent."

"Hippo?"

"Ninety-nine."

"Because nothing's a hundred percent."

"Right."

"What kind of mongoose was it that went to sleep in your shirt?"

"Banded."

"But he didn't like the bacon?"

"Only the scrambled egg."

I am looking forward to this trip more than Joe, if such

a thing is possible. I took my father to Luangwa also. He came for a fortnight; I was in the middle of a two-month sabbatical. It was shortly after my mother died; deeply healing, it was, to be surrounded by such abundance of life, by such weeds, such wilderness.

At times, I would slip out of camp and sit in the ebony glade, back to a tree, still, silent. After ten minutes this gets boring; after 20 minutes you never want to move. And I became invisible. I became another part of the forest. I had long-tailed glossy starlings going through the leaf-litter within pecking distance of my Timberlands; once a wart-hog and hoglets just beyond touching distance; once a male bushbuck I could have stroked had I wished. Well, I did wish, but I had the good manners to refrain.

Every morning, I would wake at 5.30 and put off getting up until I had identified ten birds on call. It was a process that seldom took more than 30 seconds, damn it. On my last morning, I got up in the dark. In a couple of hours before breakfast, I drank in the whole riverine panoply of Luangwa's birds. I was with Bob Stjernstedt, the cisticola man, of course. We played I Spy With My Little Ear: 30 species of bird identified on call alone. Plus six mammals identified the same way: lion, hyena, hippo, baboon, impala – these incomparably graceful and delicate gazelles bark like dogs – and best of all, a leopard, making its woodsaw roar in the glade behind camp. It was a last Luangwa symphony.

High-pitched sound is one of the first things you lose in age. An old birdwatcher famously remarked: "These days I can't hear either goldcrests or women."

And there are my father and I on another long walk. He had been suffering from sciatica, so Suffolk was a better bet than Cornwall. The hill-climbing in Suffolk is the best in the country for someone who is shaking off sciatica. We went in May, naturally. And there we were standing under a tree in which a goldcrest was singing his minute heart out. Smallest birds in Britain, with a pretty squeakingly-high little song, a lovely little jumble of golden notes. "No," my father said. "Can't get it."

"Tough. We're going to stay here until you do."

So we stayed, still and quiet, and the goldcrest, emboldened, continued his concert, filling the Suffolk sandling air with his thin and lovely little song. And then I got a smile. A nod. Got it. Bloody got it. And I showed it, I, who had been taught, had bloody well taught it back.

We walked on, a slight bounce in our stride, onwards to the next point, one that certainly involved ales. I wonder if he'll ever hear goldcrest again.

Contacts

**Royal Society
for the Protection of Birds**
The Lodge
Sandy
Bedfordshire
SG19 2DL
017676 80551
www.rspb.org.uk

**Worldwide Fund
for Nature**
Panda House
Weyside Park
Godalming
Surrey
GU7 1XR
01483 426444
www.wwf-uk.org

Birdlife International
(an international
organisation for bird
conservation)
3-4 Wellbrook Court
Girton
Cambridge
CB3 0NA
01223 277318
www.birdlife.org.uk

The Wildlife Trusts
(Umbrella organisation for
the county wildlife trusts)
The Kiln
Waterside
Mather Road
Newark
Nottinghamshire
NG24 1WT
www.wildlifetrusts.org

Wildsounds
(a commercial organisation
that supplies recordings of
bird sound, other recordings
of natural sounds; also
wildlife books)
Roses Pightle
Cross St
Salthouse
NR25 7XH
www.wildsounds.com

I'm A Teacher
Get Me Out of Here!
Francis Gilbert
1-904095-68-2

At last, here it is. The book that tells you the unvarnished truth about teaching. By turns hilarious, sobering, and downright horrifying, *I'm a Teacher, Get me Out of Here* contains the sort of information that you won't find in any school prospectus, government advert, or Hollywood film.

In this astonishing memoir, Francis Gilbert candidly describes the remarkable way in which he was trained to be a teacher, his terrifying first lesson and his even more frightening experiences in his first job at Truss comprehensive, one of the worst schools in the country.

Follow Gilbert on his rollercoaster journey through the world that is the English education system; encounter thuggish and charming children, terrible and brilliant teachers; learn about the sinister effects of school inspectors and the teacher's disease of 'controloholism'. Spy on what really goes on behind the closed doors of inner-city schools.

My Brief Career
The trials of a young lawyer
Harry Mount
1-904095-69-0

My Brief Career, Harry Mount's hilarious account of his hellish year as a "pupil" – a trainee barrister in The Temple – has all the horror of a Dickensian tragedy and all the charm of Bridget Jones' Diaries. An exposé of what goes on behind the ancient walls of London's inns of court, this fascinating story dares to reveal the grim secrets of one of England's most archaic institutions. This is a book for everyone who has ever thought they might want to become a lawyer.

The Cruel Mother
A Family Ghost Laid to Rest
Siân Busby
1-904095-71-2

In 1919 Siân Busby's great-grandmother, Bess, gave birth to triplets. One of the babies died at birth and eleven days later Bess drowned the surviving twins in a bath of cold water. She was sentenced to an indefinite term of imprisonment at Broadmoor.

The murder and the deep sense of shame it generated obviously affected Bess, her husband and their surviving children to an extraordinary degree, but it also resounded through the lives of her grandchildren and great-grandchildren. It gave rise to a collective anxiety about their family's ability to parent and an obsessive fear of hereditary insanity and depressive illness.

In Siân's case, ill-suppressed knowledge of the event manifested itself in recurring nightmares and contributed towards a prolonged bout of post-natal depression. After the birth of her second son, she decided to investigate the story once and for all and lay to rest the ghosts which have haunted the family for 80 years…

The Irresistible Con (paperback)
The bizarre life of a fraudulent genius
Francis Wheen
1-904095-74-7

His names were crazy enough – Baron Hajdu, Carl Rodgers, Mr Carl, Michael Karoly. And his jobs – receptionist, hypnotherapist, businessman, rentier, journalist and sex worker... But he was always careful to cover his tracks, so noone suspected a thing when in 1971 a curious new figure appeared on the London academic scene.

Her name was Charlotte Bach, and she was a broad-shouldered mammoth of a woman, with a deep voice and a heavy Central European accent. She was a former lecturer at the University of Budapest, and had a new theory of sex and evolution which was soon being heralded as one of the greatest intellectual advances of the 20th century...

The Irresistible Con is the gloriously bizarre story of a con-man extraordinaire, and one of Francis Wheen's funniest pieces of writing yet.

In case of difficulty in purchasing any Short Books
title through normal channels, please contact
BOOKPOST Tel: 01624 836000
Fax: 01624 837033
email: bookshop@enterprise.net
www.bookpost.co.uk
Please quote ref. 'Short Books'